ORIENTAL BARBECUES

Oriental Barbecues

Recipes and Menus
from Six Asian Countries

by
MAY WONG TRENT

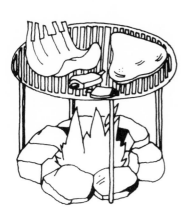

Macmillan Publishing Co., Inc.
NEW YORK

*To Michael, Junior, and
Christopher*

Macmillan Publishing Co., Inc.
866 Third Avenue, New York, N.Y. 10022
Collier-Macmillan Canada Ltd.

Library of Congress Catalog Card
Number: 73–75343
First Printing 1974

Printed in the United States of America

CONTENTS

I

COOKING OVER FIRE

ONE. *The Asian Barbecues* 9
TWO. *The Meat* 12
THREE. *The Fire* 21
FOUR. *Menu Suggestions for Complete Barbecue Dinners* 26

II

RECIPE SECTION

FIVE. *Mongolian Fire Grill* 29
SIX. *Chinese Roast Meat* 37
SEVEN. *Korean Grilled Meat* 47
EIGHT. *Japanese Yakimonos (Broiled Things)* 53
NINE. *The Indonesian Sates* 62
TEN. *Vietnamese Barbecued Meat* 72

III

Shopping Guide for Ingredients 81

INDEX 85

I
COOKING
OVER
FIRE

CHAPTER ONE
THE
ASIAN
BARBECUES

The barbecue, or cooking over fire, is the oldest form of cooking known to man. It probably originated after a forest fire when our ancestors discovered that animal meat tasted much better cooked than raw. With the passage of time, as cooking and the preparation of food became a complicated art accompanied by rigid eating manners, the barbecue became all but obsolete. Today, thanks to the Americans who are credited with popularizing outdoor cooking, the barbecue once again holds a prominent place in casual enter-taining. A patio cookout with charcoal grill, steaks, and salads can be as simple or as elegant a meal as you wish. When you become tired of steak, why not turn to the East for inspira-tion? Yes, Asian barbecues do exist. In Asia, cooking over a fire usually is a necessity rather than a change of pace, due to the lack of kitchen facilities, cooking utensils, and a very limited food budget. In some areas of Asia, electric or gas ranges, refrigeration, and shelves of pots, pans, and serving dishes do not exist. A small fire, an inexpensive cut of meat sliced and spiced, perhaps some bamboo splinters for skewers, and a bowl of rice will feed the family. In many parts of Asia one will still see natives squatting over a pit dug in the ground, cooking meals by using gathered sticks of wood as fuel, leaves as utensils, and shells as bowls. Elsewhere in affluent Asia, charcoal broiled marinated meats remain a great favorite with everyone and are the speciality of many restaurants. A barbecue can truly be said to be universal in appeal.

In recent years the world has discovered oriental cooking; and the delicacies of specialized regional cooking such as the Chinese Szechuan variety have become extremely popular. But few people have discovered the delicious and varied forms of Asian barbecues, which is odd considering the number of homes with hibachi, grill, or some sort of barbecue equipment. So let us bring out the virtues of the neglected grilled meat and acquaint ourselves with this delightful form of cooking. It is by no means similar to the "make-mine-rare" kind of barbecue. Almost without exception, the Asian barbecue, be it Mongolian, Chinese, Korean, Japanese, Indonesian, or Vietnamese, places great emphasis on the cutting and slicing of the meat, on the intricately spiced marinades that give the meat a highly seasoned taste, and on good broiling technique. The meat is crisp and brown on the outside and has the tantalizing aroma of many oriental spices. The type of barbecue varies from region to region. This book will provide you with the barbecue methods and secrets of six countries: Mongolia, China, Korea, Japan, Indonesia, and Vietnam.

MONGOLIAN FIRE GRILL

The Mongolian Fire Grill is a do-it-yourself table barbecue. Thinly sliced meat is cooked by searing briefly on a flat metal sheet over a fire. The meat, which is dipped in a special marinade just before cooking, can be sliced mutton or lamb, venison, or beef. Vegetables such as leeks and watercress can be cooked the same way as the meat, and these, with rice or bread, make a very substantial meal.

CHINESE ROAST MEAT

Meats like duck, chicken, suckling pig, pork, or spareribs are marinated in soy sauce, hoisin sauce, fresh ginger, and/or garlic. These are broiled or barbecued over a fire to give crisp, richly colored roast meat. Accompanied by rice and tea, this makes an authentic and delicious Chinese dinner for you and your guests.

KOREAN GRILLED MEAT

Thinly sliced beef, shrimps, or chicken is marinated in a soy sauce, garlic, and sesame seed mixture. It is then cooked one morsel at a time over a small table hibachi or grill, usually by the guests themselves. Rice and a pickled Korean salad called "Kim Chee" complete the dinner.

JAPANESE YAKIMONOS

Literally "broiled things," yakimono can be beef, chicken, fish, or vegetables marinated first in Japanese soy sauce and sweet sake, then grilled and served with a tart green horseradish. Most frequently the meat is cut in small cubes and threaded on skewers before broiling. An elegant Japanese dinner for company can be prepared from some of the recipes in this book, which include beef teriyaki and chicken yakitori, vinegared rice, and a spinach and sesame seed salad.

INDONESIAN SATES

The Indonesian sates are skewered cubes of lamb or pork, sliced beef, and shrimps, which have been marinated and barbecued over a fire. The marinade includes unusual spices such as turmeric, red chili powder, ground peanuts, and fresh ginger. You can plan an exotic Indonesian evening in the backyard with these recipes of lamb or shrimp sates, cold rice "longtongs," and a salad of fresh beansprouts, green cabbage, and cucumbers, which the Indonesians call "gado-gado."

VIETNAMESE BARBECUED MEAT

Very popular in France are the famous Vietnamese barbecued patties of ground meat (pork, shrimps, or fish) cooked on skewers and presented with a very interesting serving method called "wrap and eat." Fresh lettuce leaves are used as wrapping, in which are placed rice, the barbecued meat patties, fresh mint, and Chinese parsley leaves. The diner wraps the leaf up and dips it into a spicy Nuoc Mam sauce. The combination of crisp leaves and meat is delicious.

CHAPTER TWO
THE
MEAT

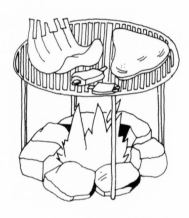

ASIAN WAYS
OF BROILING MEAT

In Asia, although there are numerous barbecued meat dishes, the different ways of broiling them are few. The variations are mainly in the marinades and sauces used in conjunction with the meat. The meats are all broiled over red-hot charcoal 3 to 4 inches from the fire. They can be broiled as they are, or skewered, spitted, or covered in leaves or foil.
SIMPLE BROILING. *The whole piece of meat is broiled 3 to 4 inches from fire, resting on an open grill. The size of the meat should be that of a serving portion (poultry is usually quartered) so that it can be turned easily on the grill. It takes about 15 to 20 minutes for each side to cook. Chinese spareribs and roast pork, Japanese teriyaki, and Korean short ribs are cooked in this way.*
SPIT BROILING. *When a large piece of meat like a whole pig (or chicken or duck), is barbecued over a fire, spitting is recommended to ensure even broiling and thorough cooking. To spit a piece of meat, pierce it on a rod or fork so that the meat can be balanced and turned over a fire. Be sure to spit through the length of the meat as near the center as possible so the weight is balanced. Secure the meat to prevent its slipping around the rod. A spit can be the simple hand-turned variety or an electric rotisserie that turns*

automatically. It takes longer to cook meat on a spit than on a grill, because in spit broiling it is turning at a distance from the fire. In this book, the suckling pig is spitted for broiling over an open fire; many other dishes such as duck, roast pork, or spareribs can also be spitted. Spitting allows the meat to broil evenly and there is less chance of it getting charred when the chef's attention is elsewhere.

ROUND TABLE BROILING. Sitting around a table the guests themselves can broil their meat on a little charcoal broiler called a "hibachi." The meat is sliced into very thin bite-size pieces. Each guest spreads one slice of meat at a time on a meshed wire grill over the charcoal. It is seared briefly and eaten hot before cooking the next piece. Korean beef (Bul Kogi) is done this way.

A variation of this method is found in the Mongolian Fire Grill. The slices of meat are seared on an oiled metal sheet over a fire (hibachi or electric ring), and not on an open meshed grill.

SKEWER BROILING. For skewer broiling the meat is cut into bite-size cubes, or long strips, or ground meat is shaped into patties, and then threaded on skewers. The skewers are then placed 3 to 4 inches from fire until the meat is crisp and brown on the outside. Skewers for threading the meat can be bamboo, wood, or metal. The

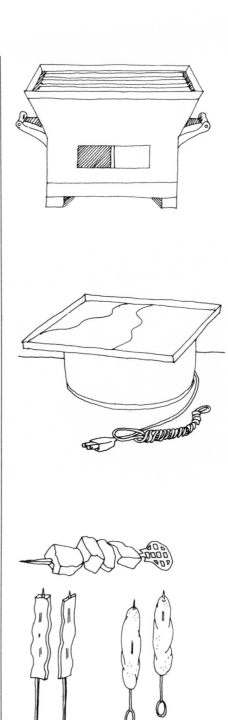

13

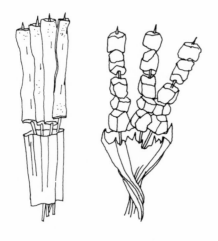

length of the skewers does not matter as long as they fit the size of the fire. Standard skewer size is 6 to 8 inches long, and 4 to 6 skewers of meat per person are an average serving. Shorter skewers are best for serving broiled cocktail tidbits. Most of the recipes in this book can be served in this way.

Often the exposed ends of skewers will get very hot or charred when the meat is broiling over a fire. The ends can be protected by covering with foil, or with banana leaves as done in Asia. Or if the cooking is over a small barbecue fire, you can arrange the skewers so that the ends hang over the edges of the grill away from the heat.

Included in the skewer broiling method are chicken yakitori, fish yaki, the sates of Indonesia, and the meat patties of Vietnam.

WRAP AND BROIL. Meat can be wrapped in banana leaves or foil and then broiled over a fire. The steam trapped inside the wrapping partially cooks the food, thus keeping the meat moist. The Indonesian broiled fish is prepared this way. The natives use banana leaves, but these can be replaced by foil. Some of the chicken or duck dishes in this book, such as the Chinese broiled chicken and the Vietnamese barbecued lemon duck, can be wrapped and cooked if you are looking for an alternative method of cooking over a fire.

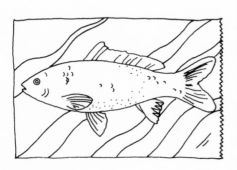

14

SUITABLE CHOICE OF MEAT

The choice of meat depends on the barbecuing methods mentioned in the preceding section. It is also limited in this book to what is suitable for the recipes from the six countries: Mongolia, China, Korea, Japan, Indonesia, and Vietnam.
The recipes call for mutton or lamb, *beef, pork, venison, shrimps, fish, chicken, and duck. The important thing to remember is that in many recipes, special cutting or slicing of the meat is called for, so only certain cuts of meat from the animal are suitable. The following is a guide to buying cuts of meat appropriate for barbecuing and the slicing called for.*

	In Simple or Spit Broiling (Whole)	In Skewer or Table Broiling (Slices)	In Skewer Broiling (Cubes)	In Skewer Broiling (Ground)
BEEF	*boneless sirloin, tenderloin, short ribs*	*flank, sirloin, or tenderloin*	*sirloin or tenderloin*	*ground round or sirloin*
LAMB OR MUTTON		*leg of, or thick chops*	*leg of, or thick chops*	*ground lean meat*
PORK	*tenderloin, spareribs*	*chops or tenderloin*	*chops or tenderloin*	*ground lean meat*
VENISON		*thick chops or steaks*		
SHRIMPS	*medium*	*medium*		*any size*
FISH	*whole snapper, sea trout*		*firm meat fillet*	*fillet*
CHICKEN	*whole or quartered*	*skinned, boned breast*	*skinned, boned breast*	
DUCK	*whole or quartered*			

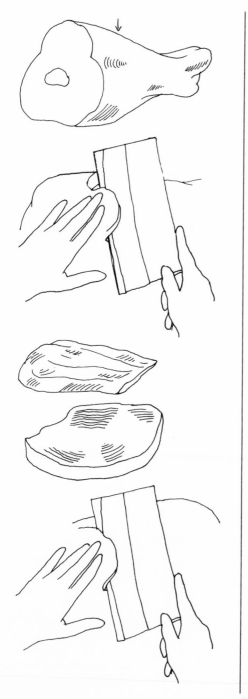

HOW TO SLICE AND CUT MEAT FOR BARBECUING

How the meat is cut and sliced, again, like its choice, depends on the five barbecuing methods mentioned at the beginning of this section. In cooking, especially in Asian cooking, the cutting and slicing of meat is most important, and instructions for it must be carefully followed to give the correct taste, texture, and appearance to the dish.

Here are step-by-step instructions and illustrations to help you on your way. The kind of knife and how you personally hold it are not important, as long as the knife is sharp, of good size, and you feel comfortable with it. The recipes in this book basically call for three major cutting methods.

(A) To cut very thin slices of meat with
as large a surface as possible:
1.   Freeze the meat half solid for
easier cutting and handling.
2.   Cut away and discard any bones,
except for a leg of lamb which you
do not need to bone.
3.   Trim and discard skin and any
fat and fibers on the meat surface,
taking care not to cut into the meat.
4.   Always slice against the grain
of the meat. (Note: "Slicing against
the grain" can be done in several
ways; the obvious one is vertically
straight down across the meat; but to
obtain larger pieces of meat, the
Asian methods include slicing down
at an angle, slicing slightly down
but outwards at a very shallow angle,
and slicing almost flat across but still
against the grain of the meat.)
5.   Start slicing some distance from
the edge of the meat. This way you
will have large pieces when you slice
out.
6.   First, make a shallow incision in
the meat with a sharp knife, the
depth will be the thickness of each
slice; then, laying the cutting edge of
the knife blade almost flat on the
incision at a very slight angle, slice
outward and cut clear of the meat.
The result is one large piece of very
thinly sliced meat.
7.   Overlap the meat on plate,
cover, and store in the refrigerator
for later use.

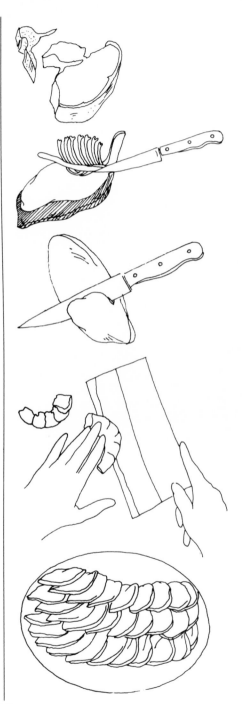

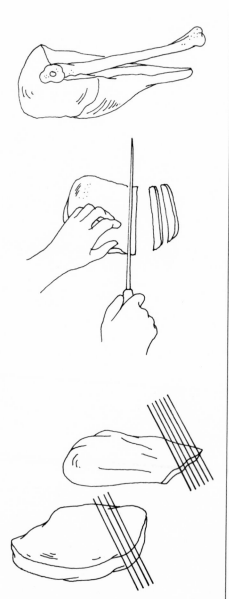

(B) To cut long thin strips of meat to thread on skewers:

1. Cut away and discard any bones.
2. Trim skin, fat, and fibers off the surface of the meat.
3. Lay the meat flat on a cutting board, cut across the meat to give long thin strips ½ to 1 inch in diameter. If strips are too thick, halve or quarter the meat lengthwise before slicing to give the right thickness.
4. The length of the strips should fit the length of skewers used. Long ones should be cut down to size, and short ones can be used in twos or threes to fill skewers.
5. Place strips of meat in a bowl (with marinade if the recipe so directs); cover until ready to use.
6. To thread meat on skewers, thread the skewers through the length of the meat, weave in and out to hold the meat securely and taut on the skewers. The meat should cover the tips of the skewers leaving about 3 to 4 inches of the skewers exposed for holding.

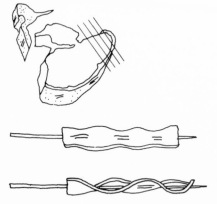

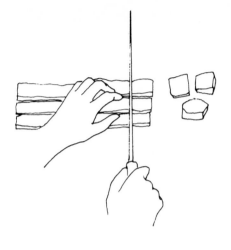

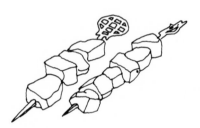

(C) To cut small cubes of meat to thread on skewers:

1. Follow exactly steps 1, 2, and 3 of method B.

2. When you have all of the ½- to 1-inch thick strips ready, cut them across into ¼- to 1-inch cubes as called for by the recipe.

3. Put the cubes in a bowl, and cover them until ready for use.

4. To thread cubes on skewers, thread the skewer through the center of the meat cube, and continue threading until the tip of the skewer is covered leaving about 3 inches exposed at the end for holding. Press the cubes of meat fairly close together to give one continuous skewer of meat. Sometimes cubes of meat are alternated in the skewer with vegetables, such as chicken with scallions in yakitori. Be sure the size of the pieces of food strung together are of the same width to give uniformity.

CHAPTER THREE
THE FIRE

EQUIPMENT

A fire underneath and a grill above are all you need to barbecue with. You could even use just a stick to hold the meat over the fire and do without the grill. However, a hardworking cook about to create a loving dinner will appreciate the modern equipment and utensils available on the market. Items such as the barbecue grill, broiler, tongs, charcoal, and lighting fluid are all reasonably priced, durable, and a convenience to outdoor cooking pleasure.

Two equipment lists are itemized below, the first covering the essentials; the second suggesting items that will be handy to have to take care of all the barbecuing needs.

ESSENTIAL. 1. *A grill, or broiler which can be any of the following: A standard portable grill, some of which are collapsible, others equipped with wheels; an oven broiler, a separate electric broiler, or an electric rotisserie; the outdoor brick or cement barbecue that many homeowners have in their yards; or (if you have one) an indoor fireplace. You may also use the popular Japanese-style grill called a "hibachi." This is a small brazier with an insulated base, receptacle for charcoal, and a grill above for the food. It is especially useful for the recipes that call for grilling at the table. In any of these units make sure the grill spaces are sufficiently small to keep the meat*

from falling through onto the coals. If possible, the broiler should also have some way of adjusting the distance between the grill and the fire. Finally, there is the campfire or one built by the seashore using rocks to hold up a makeshift grill.

2. *Fuel.* Aside from gas and electricity to run the appropriate broiling gadgets, the common fuels for barbecuing are firewood, charcoal, and briquets. For kindling the fire you can use crumpled newspapers or wood splinters, the ever-popular commercial kindling cubes or lighter fluid, or electric starter coils. Some cooks object to the commercial fluids, which they feel give the meat a bad taste. As the type of fire called for in Asian barbecues is red-hot coals long past the smoking stage, any trace of the fluid will have disappeared.

3. *Skewers,* which are necessary if the recipe calls for them. See pages 13–14 for a discussion of skewers.

USEFUL. 1. *A small portable table next to the outdoor grill to hold all the other things.*

2. *A pair of long iron tongs with insulated handle is handy to stoke the fire or rearrange the hot charcoal.*

3. *Tongs to turn the meat, which can be large forceps or special meat turners.*

4. *A pitcher or spray bottle filled with water to cool the fire.*

5. *Asbestos gloves to protect the hands from the heat and spattering grease.*

6. *Carving board and a sharp knife.*

7. *Basting brush.*

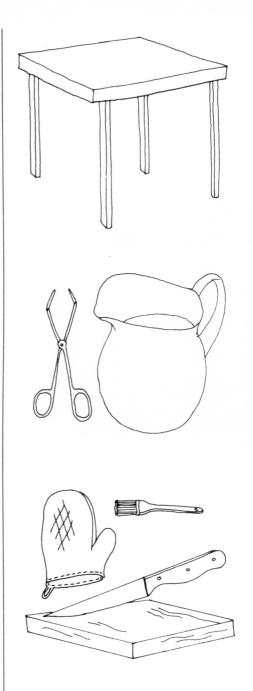

TEMPERATURE: SIZE OF FIRE AND MEAT POSITION

The cooking temperature for Asian barbecues does not have to be precise. It does not need a specific degree of heat or a meat thermometer for control. The correct cooking temperature is supplied perfectly by red-hot charcoal past the smoking stage or a high broiler flame. With this flexibility it is important to concentrate on the two main factors that determine correct cooking–the size of the fire and the position of the meat.

SIZE OF FIRE. *For the dishes discussed in this book, the size of the fire should be such that the area of burning charcoal is greater than the size of the meat being broiled. As most recipes in this book call for quick searing and a short cooking time, the fire should be of red-hot charcoal. This stage usually is reached about half an hour after initial kindling, and can be maintained for about an hour. Adding charcoal will keep the fire going longer. If the fire flares due to fat dripping from the meat or marinade, douse the flame with water from a spraying bottle.*

MEAT POSITION. *Once the meat is marinated and otherwise prepared for broiling and the charcoal is red hot, you are ready to barbecue. The only concern at this time is to be sure that the meat is positioned the right distance from the fire to give quick broiling so the meat is seared to a crispy brown while not drying its inside. For this, the meat should be not more than 3 to 4 inches away from the flame.*

COOKING TIME TABLE

Asian barbecues ask a great deal of visual judgment. The meats are usually sliced and cut into such tiny pieces that you can more easily tell they are cooked by your eyes than by meat temperature as in a large roast. For this reason, the length of cooking time cannot be precise. Moreover, timing can be thrown off balance by outside elements such as wind force, room temperature, and the size and shape of the fire at that moment. For broiling small slices, strips, or cubes of meat you are better off using your eyes as guide–a good searing is enough cooking. The cooking time table drawn up below is for the recipes in this book and should also be an adequate guide for broiling larger pieces. Be sure that the meat is thoroughly defrosted and at room temperature before starting to barbecue.

	DONENESS	
MEAT	MEDIUM (in minutes)	DONE
Beef		
1-inch steaks	*8–10*	*20*
short ribs	*15–20*	*30*
Pork		
tenderloin strips		*45–60*
spareribs		*60*
Shrimps		*10–15*
Fish		*20 (cubes)* *40–60* *(whole, wrapped)*
Chicken quarters		*40–50*
Duck		
whole		*120*
quartered		*50–60*

CHAPTER FOUR MENU SUGGESTIONS FOR COMPLETE BARBECUE DINNERS

This book is about the barbecued food of six Asian countries: Mongolia, China, Korea, Japan, Indonesia, and Vietnam. The complete dinner menus I have prepared below center around one country at a time and are planned to show its food to the best.

MONGOLIAN DINNER
Serves 6

Mongolian Fire Grill, p. 33
Rice, p. 45 or Bread
Fresh Fruit
Tea

CHINESE DINNER
Serves 6–8

Broiled Chicken, p. 41
Barbecued Spareribs, p. 43
Chinese Snow Pea Pod Salad, p. 44
Rice, p. 45
Tea

KOREAN DINNER
Serves 4

Grilled Beef Slices, p. 50
Rice, p. 45
Kim Chee Salad, p. 52
Tea

JAPANESE DINNER
Serves 6–8

Broiled Beef Teriyaki, p. 56
Broiled Fish Yaki, p. 58
Vinegared Rice, p. 60
Spinach and Sesame Seed Salad, p. 61
Tea

INDONESIAN DINNER
Serves 4–6

Lamb Sate, p. 65
Broiled Fish in Banana Leaves or Foil, p. 69
Cold Rice Longtongs, p. 68
Gado-Gado Salad, p. 70
Fresh Fruit

VIETNAMESE DINNER
Serves 4

Barbecued Skewered Pork Patties, p. 75
Lettuce Leaves
Rice, p. 45
Tea

The menus are prepared to serve varying numbers of people. You can of course double or halve the amount of food to suit your guests. Also, you can create your own menu variations by substituting other recipes within this book.

II
RECIPE
SECTION

CHAPTER FIVE
MONGOLIAN
FIRE
GRILL

The fire grill method of cooking has been known for centuries by the tough wind-swept inhabitants of Mongolia—a harsh land of lonely deserts and storm-laden mountains.

Mongolian Fire Grill uses cooking utensils that are primitive—metal sheet or pan over a fire. The meats used are game of a strong-tasting variety: goat, sheep, or deer. This is so because the Mongolians, famous as among the world's greatest horsemen, are largely nomadic groups of hunters and warriors inhabiting the vast expanse of land between North China and Siberia. The land is harsh, dry, and cold. The Mongolians raise some cattle and hunt, moving constantly in search of game. The fire grill method of cooking is ideal for this life. The day's hunt of tough game, through slicing and marinating, will be tenderized and cooked quickly over a makeshift fire. What is not eaten can be carried along without fear of spoilage because the marinade acts as a preservative. Barbecued sliced mutton, lamb, or venison is cooked on a metal sheet over a fire. A marinade of soy sauce, spices, rice wine, scallions, and Chinese parsley leaves (coriander) is used for dipping the meat into before it is placed on the hot grill to cook. The meat is eaten hot with bread or rice. Vegetables (watercress, spinach, beansprouts, leeks) are also dipped into the marinade and fried briefly on the hot grill to make a substantial meal.

This dinner, once a simple outdoor meal, has been tamed in the directions that follow and is enjoyed most sitting around a table so the guests can cook their own meal in a relaxed way. Another popular Mongolian dish is the Mongolian Fire Pot, in which sliced mutton, vegetables, and broth are all simmered in one pot over the fire. This again reflects the need of these people for quick tasty meals that are hot and nourishing and prepared with a minimum of utensils and preparation.

From the Middle Ages up to the early twentieth century, China was ruled on and off by the invading Mongolians, for example, the legendary Genghis Khan and the Manchu Dynasty. Mutton and lamb dishes were introduced to China during the Manchurian reign. Some dishes have been adapted and refined into very tasty Northern Chinese specialties. The Mongolian Fire Pot became a very elegant dinner for the ruling class. The Mongolian Fire Grill was also refined and moved indoors. Tables were specially designed with a central metal sheet heated by fire underneath, and dining à la Mongolian became a lingering event, gracious and leisurely. In Hong Kong, Taiwan, and Japan, the Mongolian Fire Grill, or "Genghis Khan dinner" as it has come to be named, has become extremely popular in recent years. Restaurants and hotels specializing in this dish have made it into an exotic dining pleasure. Frequently the decor is reminiscent of Mongolia, complete with Mongolian-costumed waiters, torches, and mountain dancers adding to the flavor. Decorations aside, it is the food itself, of course, that attracts the customers, and if you like barbecued meat with a spicy Oriental flavor, you will love the Mongolian Fire Grill. These pages offer detailed instructions on how to prepare the Mongolian Fire Grill for home entertaining. In general, all you need to know about this exotic dinner is that it is usually eaten around a table-type barbecue with sliced and marinated meats such as lamb, mutton, venison, or beef. Rice, bread, and vegetables are also served to complete the dinner. If you have a low table, throw lots of cushions on the floor, relax while you dine, and you will be transported to the days of the Manchurian court. If someone else is cooking and offering you mouthfuls of grilled meat, you are actually savoring the pampered life of a favorite courtesan inside the Imperial City during the reign of the Manchus.

SUITABLE CUTS OF MEAT
AND THE ART
OF SLICING THEM

*A good Mongolian Fire Grill depends
on the slicing of the meat. It must be*
1.   *Thin enough to cook quickly and
evenly;*
2.   *Large enough to be spread flat on
the hot metal sheet and to absorb lots
of marinade;*
3.   *Cut against the grain to give a
more tender meat and to prevent
curling when cooked.*
*Normally the Mongolians used either
mutton or lamb. Sometimes after a good
day of hunting, venison was available
and was cooked this way. Beef and camel
from their herds were also used. If you
prefer variety, chicken, shrimps, or pork
can be substituted for camel.*
*When buying the meat, choose a lean
piece in one large chunk, a whole leg
or a thick steak so that it can be cut
across the grain to yield large thin
slices. Here is a guide for buying meat:*
1.   *Mutton or lamb—whole leg section;*
2.   *Venison—go to a special game
butcher for this. Ask for cuts from the
leg or haunch section, specify lean steaks
like loin or chops in large thick pieces.
Remove all fat and fibers before slicing;*
3.   *Beef—whole flank steak, boneless
sirloin, tenderloin, or chuck in one thick
piece;*
4.   *For varieties—boned and skinned
chicken breast, lean pork (tenderloin or
chops), or shelled and deveined shrimps,
all very thinly sliced.*

SLICING

WHOLE LEG SECTION
(MUTTON, LAMB, OR VENISON).
1.   *Freeze meat half solid for easier
handling and slicing.*
2.   *Trim and discard skin, fibers, and
fat on the outside.*
3.   *Starting from the middle of the
leg, lay knife almost flat on the meat
and slice thinly at a slant right across
the grain. You should just skim the surface at an angle to give large thin slices.*
4.   *Arrange meat overlapping on several plates so that each guest can have
one plate. Cover and stack in refrigerator until ready to use.*
5.   *When the front half of the leg is
sliced to the bone, repeat procedure
on the hind part. This part has some
fibers and tendons that should be
trimmed and discarded as you come to
them.*

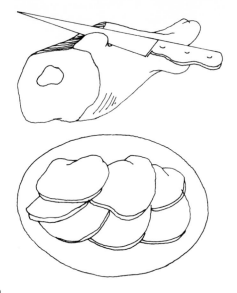

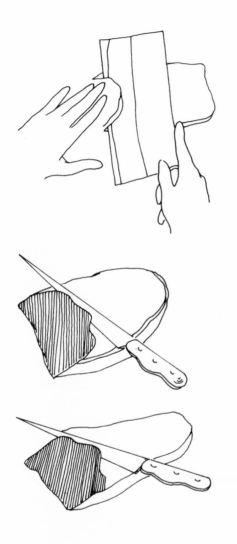

LARGE STEAKS OR CHUNKS OF MEAT (MUTTON, VENISON, BEEF, PORK). 1. *If there are any bones, trim and discard.*

2. *Follow steps 1 through 4 for leg section, using the illustrations on this page as a guide.*

Note: When meats are thick and boneless, knife position can be more vertical going down so you will automatically get a large surface area. But for easier handling and slicing, it is best to always keep the knife blade flat at an angle, and to start skimming the surface of the meat first.

For more slicing information, see pages 16–20.

MONGOLIAN FIRE GRILL
Serves 6

INGREDIENTS.
The meat:
A 5-pound leg of lamb or mutton or
3 pounds lean meat without bones in
one thick piece (lamb, beef, mutton,
venison)

The sauce:
   1½ cups dark soy
   6 cups water
   10 peppercorns, crushed
   4 star anise
   4 cloves garlic, crushed
   1 cup rice wine or sherry
   1 tablespoon sugar
   Salt to taste
   3 cups chopped scallions or leeks
   3 cups fresh parsley leaves

The vegetables:
   ½ pound watercress washed and
      cut into 2-inch pieces
   ½ pound spinach, washed and cut
      into 2-inch pieces or ½ pound
      fresh beansprouts
   ½ pound leeks, washed and cut
      into 2-inch pieces

Rice or bread (French or Middle
Eastern)

DIRECTIONS. *Trim and slice the meat. Cover with waxed paper and stack the plates of meat in the refrigerator until dinner time.*

Make the sauce in advance: Bring the soy, water, peppercorns, anise, and garlic to a simmer in a pot. Remove from heat and strain the sauce. Allow to cool. Add the wine and sugar (and salt to taste). Add 2 cups each of chopped scallions and Chinese parsley leaves, leaving 1 cup each for replenishing later on. (The scallions and Chinese parsley are the chief flavor in the Mongolian Fire Grill, and some of these should go into the grill with the meat when cooking. If Chinese parsley is not available, use both scallions and leeks. As you cook and eat, you will want to add more scallions and parsley to your sauce to maintain the flavor.) Divide sauce into 6 bowls so that each guest has his own. Place some sauce in a small pitcher to pour directly onto the sizzling meat when needed; this is optional, but useful, when the meat is burning or drying on the grill or hard to pry loose.

Wash, drain, and prepare watercress, spinach (or beansprouts) and leeks. Place in separate bowls or arrange on one large platter. (Other suitable vegetables are thinly sliced onions, green peppers, or eggplant.)

Cook the rice according to directions on page 45 a half hour before dinner, and keep warm. Serve in individual rice bowls at dinner. Or serve warmed Middle Eastern bread or a thinly sliced French loaf. The grilled meat can be sandwiched between the bread.

THE GRILL

Electric grill, electric frying pan, electric wok, or hibachi for the table
Heavy cookie sheet or large shallow skillet
1 cup cooking oil
Brush
Spatula

Place an electric grill or hibachi with burning charcoal in the middle of the table when you are ready to serve. Construct a makeshift Mongolian fire grill by placing a heavy metal cookie sheet or large shallow skillet over the heat. Do not cook on open meshed wire grill as the sauce will drip away, leaving the meat sticking to the wire. (Also you cannot cook and fry the vegetables on an open grill.) Just before dinner, heat the cooking sheet, brush with oil, and invite your guests to sit down. Now and then you scrape away charred bits of food with spatula, regrease the grill, and start afresh.

34

THE SERVING. *As this is a help-yourself type of dinner, everyone cooks for himself.*

1. *At the start the host (or hostess) brushes the hot cooking surface with oil. Throughout dinner his other chores include keeping the grill clean by now and then scraping away charred bits of food with the spatula and regreasing the grill; he can also show guests how to douse burning food with the sauce before it gets too charred to eat.*

2. *Each guest starts the meal by dipping a slice of meat into the bowl of sauce, picking up some scallions and parsley with the meat, and transferring it to the cooking sheet. Spread meat flat on grill and sear briefly on both sides.*

3. *Eat while hot. Take some rice or bread, a sip of wine, and repeat the cooking process.*

4. *At intervals, dip some watercress, spinach, or leeks into the sauce, sear on grill and eat.*

5. *Normally the guests will finish their meat first, in which case, clean and regrease the pan, place all the remaining vegetables on the grill, pour on sauce, and turn several times to stir fry. Divide portions among guests. Adding some oil while the vegetables are cooking will improve the taste.*

Serve tea and fresh fruit for dessert.

35

THE TABLE SETTING

*A square or round table is ideal so that
the grill is within easy reach of all. Each
guest has a place setting of:
A pair of chopsticks (or a fork)
A plate for the meat, bread or a rice bowl
A bowl of sauce and a plate of raw meat
Wine glass, tea cup
Also on the table to be shared by the
diners will be vegetables, the extra
pitcher of sauce, and the extra scallions
and Chinese parsley leaves. The grill
is placed in the center.*

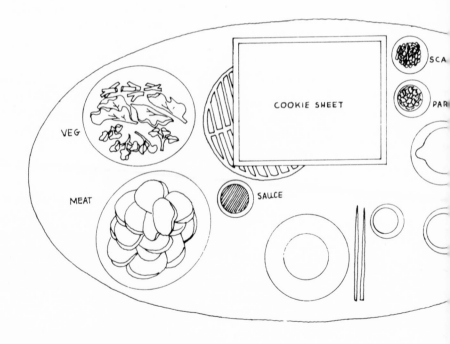

CHAPTER SIX
CHINESE
ROAST
MEAT

Chinese food has become very popular
in the United States. No one speaks
of chop suey, chow mein, or combination dinner any more. Instead, the talk
is about regional cuisine: the hot
Szechuan dishes, Hunan specialties,
classic Northern food, Fukien food,
and the stir-fry dishes of Canton.
Chinese ingredients are increasingly
available on supermarket shelves.
People are not content with just going
to Chinese restaurants or the mush-
rooming corner take-out shops. They
want to dazzle their friends with a
home-cooked Chinese dinner. The next
time you plan to cook a Chinese
dinner for your friends, why not try
a Chinese barbecue?

No Asian barbecue cookbook would be
complete without the food of China:
Chinese roast meat. This is not oven
cooked as the word "roast" suggests,
but is truly barbecued over an open
fire. In China, roast meats are
commonly sold in grocery stores or
special "cooked meats" shops, much as
cold cuts are sold in the delicatessens
in the United States. Jamming the
window displays will be roast duck,
spareribs, squids, crisp roast pigs,
grilled livers and tongue, lean pork,
chicken, squabs. You can buy any
amount, from a chicken wing, to a
duck's foot, to a whole suckling pig.
If you want just a drumstick to munch
on, they will hack it off a duck then
and there. These meats make an
excellent "emergency dish." They can
be taken home and served cold just as

they come, or reheated.

Although the suggestions here are for serving the food hot from the broiler, a cold barbecue supper cooked the day before may not be a bad idea in summer. Ironically, although the barbecue came into being when our ancestors cooked meats over a fire during their outdoor living stage, which is still true among natives in remote parts of Asia, early civilization and living indoors made this almost impossible. For example, years ago, the Chinese kitchens seldom had facilities for cooking roast meats. Fuel is precious, and a brazier would take care of all the cooking in the house. Consequently, few families would attempt to cook roast meats although it is a regular item in the menu. For this reason, the roast meat shops emerged. They were able to offer home-made roast meat at a reasonable price, and the housewives gladly welcomed this convenience. However, home barbecues are definitely coming back. In recent years, as more and more families have adequate kitchens with broiling facilities, and as most of the Chinese community in America does not live in a "Chinatown," everyone has taken to doing their own cooking. Roast strips of lean pork, especially, is a frequent ingredient in many Chinese dishes. The recipes below include roast duck, chicken, suckling pig, pork strips, and spareribs. The cooking methods are straightforward, and the ingredients are easily obtainable: dark soy,

honey, hoisin sauce, and fresh ginger. The meats used are either broiled whole or cut first into serving pieces. Some recipes call for spits which is not a problem if you have a rotisserie broiler; otherwise you spit the meat and turn it on the fire by hand. The meats are marinated beforehand. Sometimes there are two sauces: The seasoning sauce which is highly seasoned to rub all over the insides of the duck, chicken, or pig; then a basting sauce to give the outside color and to crisp it. All the preparatory work–spitting, cutting, marinating, rubbing with sauces–can be done beforehand. Establish the cooking time required, prepare the fire, and you can be sitting in front of a fire with the meat going, sipping your favorite drink by the time the guests arrive.

Chinese usually eat rice with their meals, and a recipe for plain white rice is included. This recipe will be used over and over again in this book as the basis of other rice dishes of Asia. For the vegetable dish to complete the dinner, you will find directions for a cold Chinese salad seasoned with light soy and sesame oil. Although Chinese vegetables are usually stir fried and served hot, there are a few salads that are tossed in oil and vinegar. The snow pea pod salad appearing here is an interesting addition to any salad repertoire.

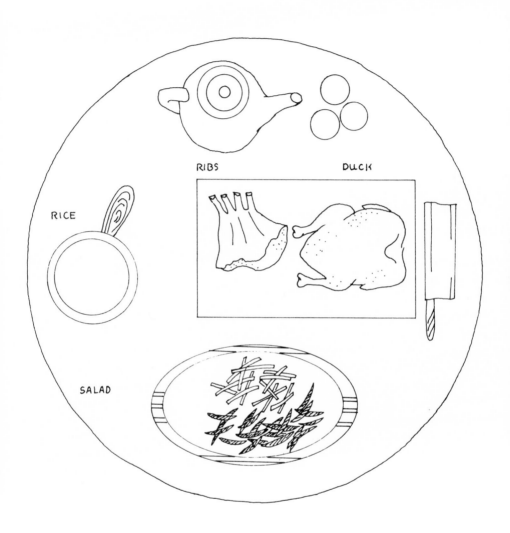

RICE

RIBS

DUCK

SALAD

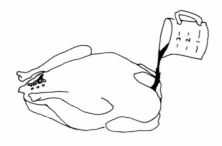

ROAST DUCK
Serves 4

INGREDIENTS.
one 4- to 6-pound duck
Seasoning sauce:
   2 cloves garlic chopped fine
   2 scallions chopped fine
   1 tablespoon oil
   3 tablespoons dark soy
   1 tablespoon sherry
   ¼ cup water
   2 star anise
   1 teaspoon sugar
   ½ teaspoon black pepper
   Salt
Basting sauce:
   3 tablespoons hoisin sauce
   1 cup water

DIRECTIONS. *Make the seasoning sauce by sautéing garlic and scallions in oil until limp. Add dark soy, sherry, water, anise, sugar, pepper, and salt to taste. Simmer 5 minutes, cool. Brush inside of duck well with this sauce, then pour any remaining sauce into the duck cavity. Keep sauce from spilling by closing skin in neck and tail with toothpicks or hooks. Make the basting sauce by combining hoisin sauce and water. Brush sauce all over duck skin. Prepare fire for barbecuing. Broil duck 3 to 4 inches from fire for 2½ hours until crisp and brown, turning and basting every 15 minutes to prevent burning.*
THE SERVING. *Pour sauce collected inside duck into a bowl for dipping. Carve duck into serving pieces and serve hot with rice and salad.*

BROILED CHICKEN
Serves 4

INGREDIENTS.
One large roasting chicken,
  quartered

Marinade:
    4 tablespoons dark soy
    1 tablespoon sherry
    4 cloves shallots, chopped fine
    1 teaspoon grated fresh ginger
    1 teaspoon sugar
    Salt to taste

    Charcoal grill, broiler, or hibachi

DIRECTIONS.   *In a large bowl make
marinade by combining soy, sherry,
shallots, ginger, sugar, and salt. Add
chicken quarters and marinate 2 hours
or longer.
Prepare fire for barbecuing. Broil chicken
skin side down first 3 to 4 inches from fire
for 30 minutes, until crisp and brown.
Turn and broil the other side 25 minutes.*
THE SERVING.   *Chicken marinated
for 3 hours will have a highly seasoned
taste. Serve hot with white rice and
Chinese salad.*

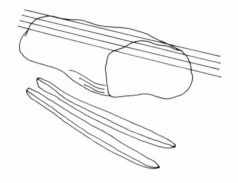

ROAST PORK STRIPS
Serves 4

INGREDIENTS.
3 pounds boneless pork tenderloin in
one piece

Marinade:
    1 teaspoon grated fresh ginger
    2 cloves garlic, chopped fine
    3 tablespoons hoisin sauce
    4 tablespoons dark soy
    1 tablespoon sherry
    1 teaspoon sugar
    Salt to taste

Charcoal grill, broiler, or hibachi

DIRECTIONS.   *Cut pork lengthwise
into four or more long strips about 1 ½
inches in diameter.*
*Make marinade by combining ginger,
garlic, hoisin sauce, soy, sherry, sugar,
and salt. Lay pork strips on a shallow pan,
pour marinade over, and let sit for 4 hours
or longer.*
Prepare fire for barbecuing.
*Place pork 3 to 4 inches from fire and
broil for 1 hour until crisp and brown.*
**Turn and baste with leftover mar-
inade** *every 15 minutes. Serve hot.*
THE SERVING.   *Cut pork into ¼-
inch slices, arrange on a platter, and
serve with rice and Chinese salad.*

BARBECUED SPARERIBS
Serves 4

INGREDIENTS.
5 to 6 pounds spareribs in one piece

Marinade:
  4 cloves garlic, chopped fine
  ½ cup hoisin sauce
  ½ cup dark soy
  2 tablespoons honey
  2 tablespoons sherry
  Salt to taste

Charcoal grill, broiler, or hibachi

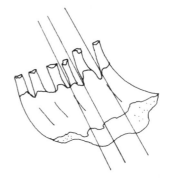

DIRECTIONS.   *Trim and discard fat
from ribs.
Prepare marinade by combining garlic,
hoisin, soy, honey, sherry, and salt. Place
spareribs on a flat pan, pour marinade
over them, and allow to sit at least 4
hours. Prepare fire for barbecuing.
Place spareribs 3 to 4 inches from fire
and broil 1 hour until crisp and brown.
Turn and baste every 15 minutes. Serve
hot or cold.*
THE SERVING.   *Cut the meat into
individual ribs and place on a platter.
Serve with rice and Chinese salad.*

CHINESE SNOW PEA PODS AND CELERY SALAD
Serves 4 to 6

INGREDIENTS.
¼ pound fresh snow pea pods,
strings removed
2 cucumbers, peeled, halved, and
seeded
1 small celery stalk, peeled and cut
into 2-inch long matchsticks

Chinese salad dressing:
4 tablespoons light soy
3 tablespoons sesame oil
4 tablespoons white vinegar
2 tablespoons oil
2 tablespoons sugar
Salt to taste

DIRECTIONS. *Bring a large pot of water to a boil. Add snow pea pods and boil 30 seconds. Rinse in cold water and drain. Cut cucumbers in ¼-inch slices and combine with the pea pods and celery.*

Make a salad dressing by combining light soy, sesame oil, white vinegar, oil, sugar, and salt. (These quantities can be varied to suit individual taste.) In a large bowl toss the vegetables and the dressing 1 hour before serving. Chill. Serve cold.

THE SERVING. *Note: Snow pea pods can be substituted with fresh broccoli cut into small 2-inch pieces, also parboiled in water for 30 seconds. (A less interesting, but nice-tasting salad can be made with just the cucumbers and the celery.)*

44

PLAIN WHITE RICE
Serves 4 to 6

INGREDIENTS.
2 cups raw white rice
3½ cups water

DIRECTIONS. *Choose a pot which has a 3 to 4 inch space left on top after the addition of rice and water so that steam can circulate.*
Wash rice 2 to 3 times until water runs clear. Drain, then add 3½ cups water. Put the rice pot, uncovered, over medium flame and bring to a boil. Boil uncovered for 5 to 6 minutes until most of the water is absorbed by the rice leaving a thin film of soaplike bubbles on the surface. Reduce flame to lowest, cover pot and cook 20 minutes. The rice is now ready to serve. It can be kept warm for ½ hour if the lid is kept on, or can be kept warm for 1 to 2 hours covered in a warm oven.

ROAST SUCKLING PIG
Serves 8 to 10

INGREDIENTS.
One 12- to 16-pound suckling pig,
  cleaned and oven ready
1 pot boiling water

Seasoning sauce:
  10 cloves garlic, mashed
  2 tablespoons 5-spice powder
  4 tablespoons dark soy
  2 tablespoons sherry
  2 tablespoons sugar
  1 teaspoon black pepper
  Salt to taste

Basting sauce:
  1½ cups water
  ½ cup white vinegar
  4 tablespoons honey or corn syrup
  2 tablespoons sherry
  aluminum foil
  2 cups hoisin sauce

DIRECTIONS. *Place pig in sink and pour boiling water over skin to scald. Dry the inside of the pig with paper towel. Make seasoning sauce by combining into a paste the garlic, 5-spice powder, dark soy, sherry, sugar, pepper, and salt. Empty sauce into pig's stomach cavity and rub all over inside of pig.*
Prepare pig for roasting by stuffing its mouth open with a ball of foil. Protect ears and tail with foil from burning. Tie legs in pairs.
Make basting sauce by bringing water to boil and adding vinegar, honey, and sherry. Cool. Half an hour before roasting

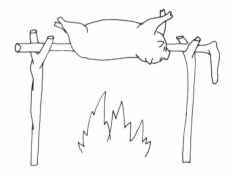

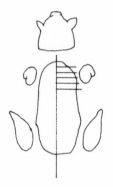

brush the entire skin of the pig with this sauce.

Meanwhile, prepare fire for barbecuing. Spit the pig and roast 4 to 6 inches from fire for about 4 hours until crisp and brown. Turn spit often for an even roast. Or roast the pig in a 350°F oven for 3 to 4 hours (about 18 minutes per pound). Place the pig on its side in a roasting pan and roast for half the time; then turn on the other side and cook until done.

THE CARVING. Remove foil from mouth, ears, and tail. If you like, decorate the head with flowers and apple. Separate head from body with a sharp knife, then cut the fore and hind legs through their joints. Separate the suckling pig into halves lengthwise by cutting down the backbone. (The bones of a suckling pig are actually quite soft. It can be hacked through with a large chopping knife, or with the help of a hammer to drive the knife through if you do not have the hacking power.) Then cut through ribs and loin to give single or double chops.

THE SERVING. Reassemble the pig more or less in its original shape on a large platter. Pass bowls of hoisin sauce to accompany meat. Serve rice or bread and a salad.

CHAPTER SEVEN
KOREAN GRILLED
MEAT

One of my favorite ways of spending a leisurely evening is to dine at a Korean grill house. The aroma of broiled meat always gives promise of a great meal to come. There is no menu, customers only indicating a choice of meat: sliced beef, pork, chicken, or shrimps. With the meat comes rice and various spicy pickled vegetable dishes called "Kim Chee." One sits at a low table; a small grill with burning charcoal is placed on it, followed by plates of marinated meat, rice, and Kim Chee. The beef, pork, or chicken is sliced very thin across the grain, shrimps are shelled, deveined, and split. The meat, or shrimp, has been marinated in dark soy, garlic, scallions, sesame seeds, and a dash of sugar. This is a do-it-yourself meal. You pick up a piece of meat with your chopsticks, and spread it out on the grill. (The grill has fine meshed wire so that the thinly sliced meat can be spread on it to cook quickly but will not fall into the fire.) Sear the meat briefly on one side, then the other to desired doneness. Eat while hot. You will love the smell of the freshly toasted sesame seeds. As the meat is very well seasoned, rice makes a good accompaniment. The side dishes of crunchy pickled turnips, cabbage, or cucumbers add to the texture and taste of the whole meal. Beer and tea are good beverages to sip throughout dinner as one gets thirsty eating grilled, seasoned meat right off the fire. The dinner is best enjoyed among two or more persons with a choice of several meats. Try either beef or chicken, and the shrimps. The just-cooked shrimps with their fragrant seared skins are delicious. After you have tried this Korean dinner yourself, you will want to repeat it for friends. Below are recipes for grilled beef (Bul Kogi) and broiled short ribs. Serve rice and Kim Chee salad and you will have a sumptuous Korean dinner.

This barbecue-type dinner is most easily cooked and served sitting down around a table with a small grill in the middle as it is impractical for one person to cook such thinly sliced meat one morsel at a time standing at a grill away from his guests. If you wish to cook outdoors for your friends, choose a larger cut of meat such as minute steak (or try broiled short ribs).

From the recipes you will notice that the Koreans cook with soy sauce, garlic, scallions, sesame seeds, and sugar. Other staples in their diet, including Chinese celery cabbage, squash, rice, seaweeds, and dry salted fish, suggest that Korean food is a combination of Chinese and Japanese elements. This is true in part: Korea is a peninsula with China in the west, and the Japanese occupied Korea in earlier times. Both China and Japan played a large part in shaping Korean culture and history. But Korea, "the peaceful kingdom," with rich valleys and fields nestling beneath soaring mountains, is also a very individual nation in terms of food. The Koreans, for example, drink far less tea than their neighbors, preferring barley water, rice water, and ginseng tea. Ginseng from Korea is the best of its kind and very much sought after. This expensive rejuvenating cure-all root is one of Korea's most renowned products.

Although there is much Korean food with its own characteristics: the Angel Pot (meat, seafood, and vegetables simmered in a broth), the Watchman's dinner (sliced meat, egg, vegetables, and mushrooms wrapped in thin pancakes), and Mandoo (meat-filled dumplings in soup); the most typical Korean dishes are Kim Chee pickles and charcoal broiled meat cooked on a Hwa Ru (table grill). Recipes follow for these dishes.

The Koreans are extremely hospitable people and the mood of their mealtime will be felt in your home as you cook the delicious Bul Kogi around a table. This leisurely round-table barbecue combines delicious food and a relaxed atmosphere for conversation.

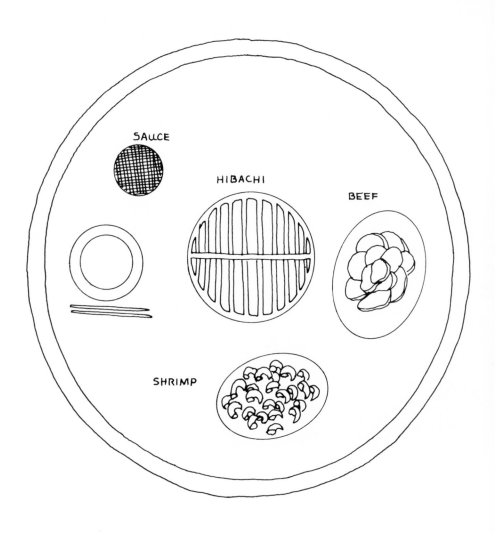

SAUCE

HIBACHI

BEEF

SHRIMP

GRILLED BEEF SLICES
(BUL KOGI)
Serves 4

INGREDIENTS.
2 pounds boneless 1- to 2-inch thick
  steak—sirloin, chuck, or flank

Marinade:
  4 scallions, chopped fine
  4 cloves garlic, mashed
  ½ cup dark soy
  2 tablespoons oil
  2 tablespoons sugar
  2 tablespoons sherry
  2 tablespoons roasted white sesame
    seeds
  Salt and black pepper

Charcoal grill or hibachi

DIRECTIONS. *Slice the beef thinly
across the grain into ¼-inch pieces (see
page 17).*
*Make the marinade by combining scal-
lions, garlic, dark soy, oil, sugar, sherry,
sesame, salt, and pepper. Add beef slices
and marinate for 1 hour or longer.*
*Prepare the fire for grilling. When the
coals are ready, place the hibachi in the
center of the table and seat your guests.
Each person cooks his own dinner by lifting a slice of beef with chopsticks or fork,
laying it flat on the grill.*
*After the meat has been seared briefly on
both sides to desired doneness, it is removed and eaten while hot and the next
slice is similarly prepared.*

THE SERVING. *Serve individual bowls of rice at beginning of meal so that the meat and rice can be enjoyed together. Kim Chee salad and beer or tea complete the dinner.*
Serve fresh fruits like apples, pears, and peaches which are abundant in Korea. Note: The other meats used in the Korean grill are thinly sliced chicken breast, pork thinly sliced, and shrimps that have been shelled, deveined, and halved lengthwise. Marinate and broil as above. Substitute sliced beef with minute steaks if you are cooking outdoors as they are bigger and easier to handle.

GRILLED KOREAN SHORT RIBS
Serves 6

INGREDIENTS.
6 large lean short ribs

Marinade:
1 teaspoon grated fresh ginger
4 cloves garlic, mashed
2 tablespoons sugar
2 tablespoons oil
2 scallions, chopped fine
2 tablespoons roasted white sesame seeds
½ cup dark soy
Dash salt and black pepper

Charcoal grill, broiler, or hibachi

DIRECTIONS. *Trim fat from ribs. Score meat deeply with sharp knife at ½-inch intervals crosswise and once along its length. This will allow the meat to marinate and cook better.*
Make marinade by combining ginger, garlic, sugar, oil, scallions, sesame seeds, soy, salt, and pepper. Pour over ribs and marinate 2 hours or longer. Baste often. Prepare fire for barbecuing. Broil ribs 3 to 4 inches from fire 8 to 10 minutes each side until crisp and brown. Serve hot.
THE SERVING. *Serve ribs accompanied by rice and Kim Chee salad. This meal is best eaten with the fingers. Save the bones to make soup stock as do the Koreans for their many varieties of soups.*

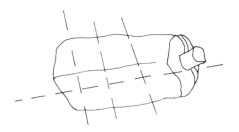

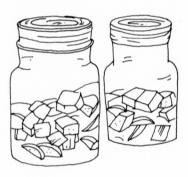

KIM CHEE SALAD
Serves 6

INGREDIENTS.
1 whole Chinese celery cabbage,
 about 2 pounds
2 Chinese turnips or cucumbers
4 cups water   ¼ cup salt
Dressing:
 2 cloves garlic, mashed
 1 teaspoon grated fresh ginger
 1 tablespoon sugar
 4 tablespoons sesame oil
 4 scallions, white parts only,
  chopped fine
 1 to 2 teaspoons crushed red pepper flakes
 4 tablespoons white vinegar

DIRECTIONS. *Wash cabbage, separate, and cut leaves into 2-inch squares. Peel, halve, and slice turnip (or seeded cucumber) very thin. Put vegetables in a large jar, add water and salt. Cover and pickle 24 hours in the refrigerator.*

THE SERVING. *Make dressing by combining garlic, ginger, sugar, oil, scallions, red pepper, and vinegar (vary amount of sugar and vinegar to taste). Drain vegetables from jar, toss with dressing, and serve. Note: Kim Chee means "pickled vegetables" and there are many varieties. The purest form is pickled Chinese celery cabbage or turnip. For this, use the above recipe but omit oil and vinegar, and pickle for 2-3 days at room temp after adding the dressing. The jar can then be stored for months in a cool place. Made this way Kim Chee is very strong and is what is served in Korea at every meal with rice. The Kim Chee salad in the recipe above is much lighter.*

CHAPTER EIGHT
JAPANESE
YAKIMONOS
(BROILED
THINGS)

Japan, land of the rising sun, is a long chain of islands lying east of China in the north Pacific. Its surrounding sea is very rich with fish, seafood, and seaweed. This marine life forms an important part of the Japanese diet, supplemented by rice, fresh vegetables such as radish, carrots, cucumbers, bamboo shoots, and a delicious mushroom which, in season, can grow to giant size. Basic meats are chicken, beef, and pork, with the famous Kobe beef now being considered by many to be the best in the world. Kobe steers are massaged daily and fed beer to give a tender marbled meat. Among the many fresh fruits are persimmons and huge strawberries, which with green tea make an ideal end to a harmonized Japanese meal.

Harmony is the keynote to all Japanese food, taking into consideration the season, the scenery, the tableware, and the presentation of the food. The result is very fresh food that is esthetic, neat, and appealing, reminiscent of other aspects of the Shinto religion.

The Japanese cook with relatively few ingredients. Soy sauce, soy bean paste, sweet sake, rice vinegar, and sesame oil are the basics. Sugar is often used to give the food a sweet taste. (In the recipes you should follow your own preference in the amount of sugar used.) Pickles, seaweeds, dried fish flakes, monosodium glutamate, and a tart green horseradish paste or hot mustard give the seasoning to soup, meat, and rice. Japanese foods have tongue-twisting names like sukiyaki, tempura, sashimi, sushi, and teriyaki. Perhaps this is one reason that despite their growing popularity in restaurants many people shy away from trying to cook these dishes. Because they really are easy to prepare, we shall discuss some of the more popular dishes. The barbecued variety of Japanese food is called "Yakimono" (Yaki, broiled; mono, things). The most popular version of Yakimono is called "Teriyaki" (teri, sunny, with a glaze; yaki, broiled). In addition there is "yakitori" (tori, chicken), fish yaki, and broiled vegetables, thus making any of the above mentioned dishes the "main" course if you are having only one dish.

In the busy shopping and theater areas in Japanese cities are stalls and restaurants serving these broiled foods only. The counters are jammed with people enjoying a quick meal of broiled beef, chicken, fish, shrimps, or squids from the hibachis piled with food at various stages of cooking.

The Japanese use a special table broiler for this type of cooking called "hibachi" in which a few pieces of red-hot charcoal will cook the food for the whole family. Every home has one for broiling, one-pot simmering, making tea, or warming food. Hibachis are becoming popular in the United States because of their efficient construction. Unlike the larger barbecue grills, they may be easily moved and placed on a dining table.

The meat in yakimono cooking can be broiled plain or with a sauce. When the sauce is made of soy sauce, sweet sake, and sugar, it gives the broiled meat a shiny glaze as well as a rich brown color. This is teri (sunny)-yaki. Below are recipes for beef teriyaki as well as for fish, shrimps, chicken, and vegetables. They will all have different tastes due to variation in the seasonings. Included also are recipes for vinegared rice and spinach-sesame seed salad to complete a Japanese dinner.

The Japanese sip and enjoy tea all day and on every occasion; with it they greet guests, transact business, linger through dinner, relax, and contemplate. The Japanese tea is green; its pale and delicate brew is distinctly different from the black or mixed teas of other countries. The new green tea leaves that are picked in May are known as "Sincha," new tea, and it is highly recommended. Tea lovers journey to the tea-growing area every year to savor the mellow brew of the fresh leaves. A second, later picking is known as "Bancha." This is the tea sipped daily at home, at places of business, and in restaurants. The famous tea ceremony uses a finely ground green tea in powder form. To brew green tea, bring water to a boil in a kettle; add 3 to 4 tablespoons of green tea to a 6- to 8-cup teapot; pour boiling water over the tea, cover, and let steep for 10 minutes. Serve it very hot. The green tea is sipped hot, without sugar or cream. A strainer is not necessary as tea leaves in the bottom of the cup are customary.

In yaki cooking, the meats need to be cut to the correct size as specified in each recipe. Some are cubed and skewered as in chicken yakitori, some are broiled whole as are the thin beef steaks in beef teriyaki. All the recipes use Japanese soy sauce to give the meat its traditional taste. The teriyaki sauce is used for dipping the meat into just before broiling, for basting, and it sometimes ends up as a glaze to spoon over the cooked meat. Unlike most Asian barbecues, the meat is not marinated for hours beforehand, which gives a unique combination of seasoning and fresh meat flavor. The cooked meat is served hot with a dab of hot green horseradish paste or English mustard. When planning a yakimono dinner, make the vinegared rice and spinach salad beforehand to serve at room temperature. Prepare the meat, sauce, and grill ahead of time and you will have little to do after your guests arrive. A buffet-style table can be set with bamboo wares, rattan mats, lacquer bowls (and perhaps a Japanese fan) to give the right atmosphere. Or if you have individual lacquer trays, lay out a complete dinner on each tray per guest; use small bowls for the rice and salad, a flat plate for the meat, and small tea cups for hot green

tea. You may even want to include a scented hot towel (as would be done in a Japanese home). These are easily prepared by bringing a pot of water to a boil. Remove the water from heat and add a few drops of light cologne. Place terrycloth hand towels in the sink and pour the scented hot water over them. Wring the towels dry and fold them into neat rectangles. Present to the guests while hot. Or prepare ahead of time and cover in foil to keep warm in the oven until dinner.

You may want to serve the popular Japanese sake wine with your meal. Sake is made from distilling fermented rice. It is usually served warmed to body temperature. Its slightly sweet taste and pale color can be compared to a medium or dry sherry, its alcohol content is that of table wine. Sake can be bought in large liquor stores in the United States. Be sure to distinguish between the pale drinking sake and the darker very sweet "mirin" sake used in cooking. There are special sake vases to hold sake while the vase is placed in a bowl of hot water.

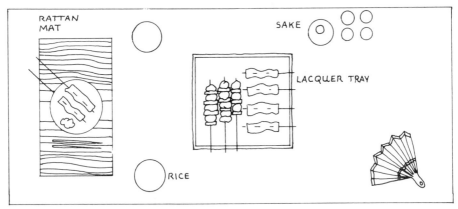

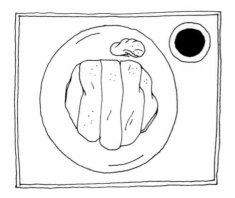

BROILED BEEF TERIYAKI
Serves 4

INGREDIENTS.
2 pounds ½- to 1-inch thick sirloin or
    tenderloin steak

Marinade:
    ½ cup Japanese soy sauce
    ¼ cup sweet sake wine or sherry
    1 to 2 tablespoons sugar
    4 cloves garlic, mashed

2 tablespoons Japanese horseradish
    powder or mustard powder
1 teaspoon cornstarch

Charcoal grill, broiler, or hibachi

DIRECTIONS. *Make marinade by
combining soy, wine, sugar, and garlic in
a pot and simmer 1 minute. Cool.
One half hour before dinner make a thick
paste with horseradish or mustard powder and hot water.
Prepare fire for barbecuing. Dip the
thin steaks into the marinade, coat well,
and broil 3 to 4 inches from fire, 2 to 3
minutes on each side until brown.
Meanwhile, make a glazing sauce by
straining the remaining marinade, dis-
solve cornstarch in it, and simmer 1 minute to thicken.*
THE SERVING. *Slice steaks into 1-
inch strips, place equal amount on each
plate, spoon glazing sauce over. Place a
dab of horseradish paste on the side and
serve the meat hot. Serve vinegared rice
and spinach salad with this dinner.*

BROILED CHICKEN YAKITORI
Serves 4

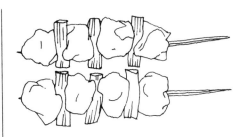

INGREDIENTS.
3 whole chicken breasts, boned and
   skinned (page 7)
6 scallions, white parts only, cut into
   1-inch lengths

Marinade:
   ½ cup Japanese soy sauce
   ¼ cup sweet sake wine or sherry
   1 teaspoon grated fresh ginger
   ½ to 1 tablespoon sugar
   ¼ cup water
Skewers
Charcoal grill, broiler, or hibachi

DIRECTIONS. *Cut chicken breasts
into 1-inch cubes. Thread skewers alter-
nating 1 piece scallion with 2 meat cubes.
Make marinade by combining soy, wine,
ginger, sugar, and water in a pot and
simmer 1 minute. Cool.
Prepare fire for barbecuing. Dip
skewers into marinade to coat well. Broil
3 to 4 inches from fire, 4 to 5 minutes on
each side until crisp and brown. Baste
twice while broiling to keep meat very
moist. (You may baste by lifting the skewers from the fire and briefly submerging
them in the marinade, then immediately
returning to the fire.)
Serve hot.*

THE SERVING. *Serve hot with vinegared rice and spinach salad. Note:
Usually chicken livers, cleaned and
halved, are alternated between scallions
and chicken in broiling. Try this if you
prefer more variety.*

57

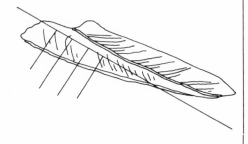

BROILED FISH YAKI
Serves 4

INGREDIENTS.
2 pounds fillet of mackerel, tuna, or
  pompano cut into 2-inch cubes

Marinade:
  ½ cup Japanese soy sauce
  ¼ cup sweet sake wine or sherry
  ½ to 1 tablespoon sugar
  1 teaspoon grated fresh ginger
  Dash white pepper

Skewers
Charcoal grill, broiler, or hibachi

.DIRECTIONS. *Make marinade by
combining soy, wine, sugar, ginger, and
pepper. Thread meat on skewers, place
in a shallow pan. Half hour before cooking pour marinade over fish.
Prepare fire for barbecuing. Place skewers 3 to 4 inches from heat and broil 4
minutes on each side or until meat is
crisp and brown. Baste twice during
cooking.
Serve hot.*
THE SERVING. *Place broiled meat
on a platter and serve with vinegared
rice and spinach salad. Pass horseradish
paste, if you wish.
Note: For other seafood yaki, substitute
2 pounds of fish with 2 pounds of scallops
medium shrimps shelled and deveined.*

58

BROILED VEGETABLES ON SKEWERS

Serves 4

INGREDIENTS.

16 fresh mushroom caps

2 green peppers, cut into 2-inch
   pieces

1 eggplant or yellow summer squash
   or zucchini, cut into 2- by 2½-inch
   cubes

4 scallions, white parts only, cut into
   2-inch lengths

Marinade:
   ½ cup Japanese soy sauce
   2 tablespoons sugar
   ¼ cup water
   2 tablespoons oil
   Dash salt

Skewers

Charcoal grill, broiler, or hibachi

DIRECTIONS. *Make marinade by combining soy, sugar, water, oil, and salt. Thread vegetables on skewers and prepare fire for barbecuing.*

Dip vegetables in marinade to coat well, broil 3 to 4 inches from fire 3 to 4 minutes each side until lightly brown. Baste twice while cooking.

Serve hot.

THE SERVING. *Serve with beef, chicken, or seafood teriyaki, rice and/or salad.*

Note: Other vegetables suitable for broiling are fresh asparagus or string beans cut into 2-inch lengths. If you prefer the vegetables less crunchy than the Japanese, you may parboil them briefly before broiling.

VINEGARED RICE
Serves 4-6

INGREDIENTS.
2 cups raw white rice

Vinegar dressing:
    4 tablespoons white vinegar
    2 tablespoons sweet sake wine or
      sherry
    Dash sugar
    Salt to taste

DIRECTIONS. *Cook rice according to recipe on page 45.*
Make vinegar dressing by combining white vinegar, wine, sugar, and salt. Add to the hot rice and mix thoroughly. Cool to room temperature and serve.
THE SERVING. *Serve with Japanese broiled meat and a salad. Note: To dress up the vinegared rice you may want to add 2 to 3 sheets of crumbled Japanese Nori seaweed to rice when mixing with the vinegar dressing to give taste and color.*

SPINACH AND
SESAME SEED SALAD
Serves 4

INGREDIENTS.
A large pot of boiling water
1 tablespoon salt
1 pound fresh spinach with rough
  stems removed, washed thoroughly

Dressing:
  2 tablespoons Japanese soy sauce
  1 tablespoon sugar
  2 tablespoons white vinegar
  2 tablespoons oil
  Salt to taste
  2 tablespoons roasted white sesame
    seeds

DIRECTIONS. *Bring the water and
salt to a rolling boil. Add spinach and
boil 1 minute. Drain, rinse in cold water,
and drain. Squeeze spinach leaves dry
from excess water. Cut into 2-inch
lengths.*
*Make salad dressing by combining soy,
sugar, vinegar, oil, and salt.*
*If sesame seeds are not roasted, toast
in oven or over medium flame on a dry
frying pan until light brown.*
THE SERVING. *One hour before
serving, toss spinach, dressing, and sesame seeds together. Serve at room temperature in individual bowls for each
guest.*

CHAPTER NINE
THE
INDONESIAN
SATES

Bali, Java, Sumatra, batik prints, teak carving, spices from the East Indies–all these, and more, are Indonesian. Ranking among one of the ten most populous areas in the world, geographically Indonesia is made up of a large collection of islands situated along the equator between the Asian mainland and Australia. For centuries, Indonesia has been a crossroad for its adventurous Asian neighbors. They came to trade and to settle, adding their different cultures to make Indonesia what it is today. This influence is seen especially in its cuisine. The early Chinese traders brought their tradition of rice, stir-fry dishes, soy sauce, and ginger. Their utensils were bowls and chopsticks. With the introduction of the Hindu and Islamic religions from India and the Middle East came curry dishes, kabob cooking, and finger eating. The Dutch during their colonial rule popularized beer drinking, and invented the colorful rijst-tafel (literally rice table). This is a buffet table ladened with various spiced meat dishes, curries, rice, and garnishes which the affluent Dutch presented their guests "native style" as a change to their own cuisine. From these diverse influences Indonesian culture finally emerged and has become a strong contender among the most spicy and exotic foods of the world.
Refined Indonesian fare naturally leans heavily on its native herbs and spices including chilis, turmeric, tamarind, coconut milk, ginger, lemon and lime, peanuts and macadamia nuts, shallots, coriander, soy sauce, and shrimp paste.

There are rice dishes wrapped in banana leaves and boiled or steamed over water, or simmered in coconut milk, sometimes brightly colored with turmeric; the curries are milder than the Indian variety, tamed with coconut milk to give a sauce that is both smooth and tingling. Served with almost every meal is the fiery Indonesian signature, sambal sauce. This is a chili and spice sauce that can have a base of coconut milk, or shrimp, fish, or soy. It goes over everything not unlike the way some people use mustard or tabasco. When used correctly, the sambal sauces arouse the taste buds and enhance the flavor of food.

With the spicy food, the Indonesians serve various cooling salads of beansprouts, beans, cabbage, and cucumber, tossed in a sweet chili and vinegar dressing flavored with ground peanuts. The recipe for the popular gado-gado salad with its nutty flavor is included here. But among the dishes in Indonesian cuisine, none can challenge the sates (pronounced satays) as the most national food of all. Every village and home has its own secret recipe for the grilled marinated morsels of meat on skewers called "sates."

It is sold, eaten, and enjoyed everywhere and at all hours of the day. It can be a simple snack from the makeshift stove of a street vendor, a casual dinner at home where everyone strings and broils their own sates around a fire, or an elaborate meal in a fancy restaurant where the sates are kept warm on little individual braziers on the table as the guests sip wine and nibble pieces of cooling cucumber between mouthfuls of pork, shrimp, beef, or chicken sates.

Sates may differ in shape and taste depending on choice of meat and its seasoning, but they all have the same basic methods of cooking and serving. First there are the small pieces of meat, then a marinade, skewers to string the seasoned meat, and a fire on which to broil it, and last a dipping sauce as the final accompaniment.

The meat can be beef, chicken, shrimp, fish, or pork. It is cut in small chunks or strips, marinated, strung on skewers, and grilled over a fire until crisp on the outside and succulent within. The coals of the fire should be red hot and past the smoking stage. If using a broiler, the meat should be about 3 to 4 inches from it for a quick but not charred grilling. When the sates are done, you should hold the end of the skewer and dip the meat in a sate peanut sauce, then eat by sliding the meat off the stick with the teeth. The dipping sauce is served in flat plates so that the hot sates can easily be rolled in it.

Rice and salad complement a sate dinner perfectly. The Indonesians would serve the gado-gado salad and a cold rice called "longtongs." Longtongs are individual packets of rice in banana leaves,

cooked in boiling water, or
steamed over it, and cooled. A
recipe for this is included here
with a suggestion for serving if
banana leaves are not available.
A sate dinner lets a hostess truly
enjoy herself during the party.
The meat is cut and marinated in
advance; the hostess can string
it on skewers beforehand or leave
it for the guests to string right at
the table. All that needs to be done
as dinnertime approaches is to
prepare a fire or bring a hibachi
to the table or light the broiler.
The rest of the dinner, namely rice
and salad, are also prepared
beforehand. What could be more
simple?
The imaginative hostess can
easily create an exotic Indonesian
evening around the food. Cover
the table with a batik cloth or a
flower fabric; use lots of big green
leaves, and wooden bowls, earthenware,
coconut shells or straw utensils to
hold the food. Is there a carved
mask or coconut shell in the house
that can be used as a centerpiece?
Place the salad in wooden bowls,
rice in leaves, meat in clay pots,
or lay a bed of leaves in a bowl
before arranging the meat inside.
(Have more leaves ready to
protect the exposed skewer ends
while broiling. City folks can use
lettuce or green cabbage leaves
for this.)
Below is a sketch of table setting
prepared for sate cooking.

GADO GADO SALAD

SKEWERS

HIBACHI

MEAT

LONTONGS' RICE

SAUCE

PLATES

SATES ON LEAVES

*In Indonesia, sates are really
the most simple native method of
cooking and a kitchen is often only
a space with an open brazier,
some firewood, and a few pots. A
standard kitchen in the Western
sense is rare, hence Indonesian
cuisine consists of many dishes
that are barbecued, or wrapped
in the leaves that serve as cooking
utensils. Thus it is natural that
sates are so extremely popular. A
few splinters of split bamboo as
skewers, a slab of meat, spices, an
open fire, and a very satisfying
meal is at hand.*

*As you savor a sate, picture a
wandering Indonesian sate
vendor: across his shoulder rests
a bamboo pole balanced by a
stove on one end and a basket on
the other. The basket contains the
meat, skewers, and secret sate
sauce. As he moves through a
village or marketplace, he calls
out his wares. As customers stroll
over, he lowers his load, kindles
the little stove, strings the meat,
and soon the aroma of freshly
broiled sates is wafting through
the air.*

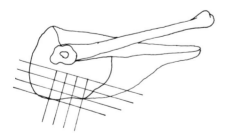

LAMB SATE
Serves 4 (makes about 20 skewers)

INGREDIENTS.
1½ pounds boneless leg of lamb,
  cut into ½-inch cubes

Marinade:
  4 tablespoons dark soy
  2 tablespoons lemon juice
  2 cloves garlic, chopped fine
  1 teaspoon grated fresh ginger
  2 teaspoons ground chili powder
  1 teaspoon brown sugar
  Salt to taste

20 skewers
Barbecue grill, broiler, or hibachi

DIRECTIONS. *Trim, bone, and cut
lamb into ½-inch cubes (page 19–20).
Make the marinade by combining
dark soy, lemon juice, garlic, ginger,
chili powder, sugar, and salt. Add
cubed lamb and marinate 2 hours
or longer.*

*Thread meat on skewers, about
3 to 4 cubes per skewer.*

*Prepare fire for barbecuing. Place
the lamb sates 3 to 4 inches from
fire and broil 5 minutes on each side
until crisp and brown on the outside.
Serve hot at once.*

THE SERVING. *Pass bowls of sate
peanut sauce (page 71) for dipping the
lamb. Serve also cold rice longtongs
(page 68) and gado-gado salad
(page 70).*

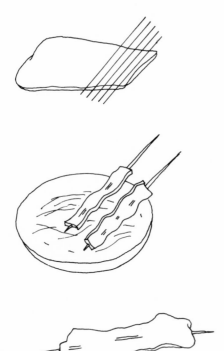

BEEF SATE

Serves 6 (makes about 30 sates)

INGREDIENTS.

2 pounds flank steak

Marinade:

    1 cup finely chopped onion
    4 cloves garlic, chopped fine
    1 teaspoon grated fresh ginger
    4 tablespoons oil
    4 teaspoons ground chili powder
    2 teaspoons turmeric powder
    1 tablespoon peanut butter
    1 teaspoon brown sugar
    ¼ teaspoon grated lemon rind
    ¾ cup water
    Salt to taste

30 skewers
Barbecue grill, broiler, or hibachi

DIRECTIONS. *Slice flank steak a-cross into ¼-inch strips (page 17). Sauté onions, garlic, and fresh ginger in oil until limp. Add chili powder, turmeric, peanut butter, brown sugar, lemon rind, water, and salt. Stir to a smooth paste and simmer 2 minutes. Add beef and simmer 3 minutes, stirring all the time. Leave mixture to cool.*
Thread meat on skewers.
Prepare fire for barbecuing. Place beef sates 3 to 4 inches from fire and broil 3 minutes each side. Meat should be crisp and brown on outside. Baste once with marinade left in bowl, if any.
THE SERVING. *Serve alone, or with sate peanut sauce, accompanied by cold rice longtongs and salad.*

66

SHRIMP SATE
Serves 4 (makes 12 skewers)

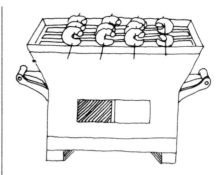

INGREDIENTS.
3 dozen medium shrimps, shelled
  and deveined

Marinade:
  4 cloves garlic, chopped fine
  2 tablespoons oil
  3 tablespoons peanut butter
  ¼ cup lemon juice
  1 teaspoon ground chili powder
  1 teaspoon turmeric powder
  Salt to taste

12 skewers
Barbecue grill, broiler, or hibachi

DIRECTIONS. *Sauté garlic in*
oil until limp. Add peanut
butter, lemon juice, chili powder,
turmeric, and salt. Stir to a smooth
paste and simmer 1 minute. Cool,
add shrimps, and stir. Marinate 1 hour
or longer.
Thread 3 shrimps to a skewer.
Prepare fire for barbecuing. Place
the shrimp sates 3 to 4 inches from
fire and broil 3 to 4 minutes each
side until crisp and brown on the
outside.
Serve hot at once.
THE SERVING. *Pass bowls of sate*
peanut sauce to dip shrimps in,
accompanied by cold rice longtongs
and gado-gado salad.

BROILED FISH IN BANANA LEAVES OR FOIL

Serves 4

INGREDIENTS.
2 to 3 pounds whole fish (snapper,
sea trout, pompano, or sea bass),
   cleaned and scaled
4 scallions cut into 2-inch lengths
Salt and pepper

Sauce:
   1 cup finely chopped onions
   2 cloves garlic, chopped fine
   2 teaspoons grated fresh ginger
   2 tablespoons oil
   1 tablespoon peanut butter
   1 teaspoon ground chili powder
   1 teaspoon turmeric powder
   1 teaspoon basil
   Juice and grated rind of 1 lemon

Banana leaves or foil for wrapping
fish
Barbecue grill or broiler
DIRECTIONS. *Wash and pat dry
fish; cut 4 shallow gashes on both sides.
Make the sauce by sautéing onions,
garlic, and ginger in oil until limp,
then make a smooth paste by adding
peanut butter, chili powder,
turmeric, basil, and lemon juice
and rind.*
*Place overlapping layers of banana
leaves or tin foil on table, spread
a thin layer of half the scallions on
it, cover with half of the sauce. Add
fish, season well with salt and
pepper, spread remaining scallions
and sauce on top. Wrap fish securely,
tucking and folding corners of
leaves or foil. Tie with string.*

*Prepare fire for broiling, broil fish
25 minutes either side. Serve hot at
once.*
THE SERVING. *Unwrap fish, divide
into four portions, and serve with
its sauce. Serve plain rice and a salad
with it.*

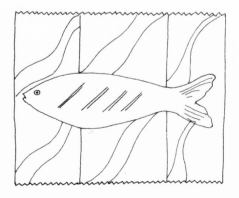

68

RICE IN BANANA LEAVES (LONGTONGS)
Makes 8 packets

INGREDIENTS.
2 cups white rice, washed and
  drained
8 pieces banana leaves 10 by 10
  inches

Strings to tie
1 large pot boiling water

DIRECTIONS. *Arrange banana
leaves flat on table, place ¼ cup rice in
middle of each leaf, fold each leaf securely into a rectangular 3- by 6-inch
packet. Tie with string so that no grains
of rice can escape.
Immerse packets of rice in a large
pot of boiling water. Reduce heat and
simmer 1 hour.
Or steam packets of rice in a covered
pot of boiling water for 1 hour. As
the rice is cooked it expands to fill
the whole packet.
Discard strings, and cool rice in its
packet without unwrapping.*
THE SERVING. *Serve cold at room
temperature, 1 packet per guest.
Unfold leaves to eat.
These rice packets are called "longtongs," and can be cooked 1 to 2 days
in advance and kept in the refrigerator.
If banana leaves are not available,
cook plain rice (page 45). Use an
ice cream scoop or ladle to make rice
balls while rice is hot. Pack rice
tightly and unmold to cool.
Pick green leaves from garden or
use lettuce or green cabbage leaves,
wash and line a large tray, and place
cold rice balls on it.
Or wrap rice balls with leaves and
secure with toothpicks. Whichever
way you do it, the idea is to serve
cold rice in individual packets.*

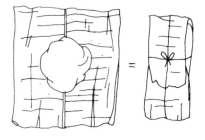

69

GADO-GADO SALAD WITH PEANUT DRESSING
Serves 6 to 8

INGREDIENTS.
½ pound fresh beansprouts, washed
    and drained
½ pound green beans, cut into 2-inch
    pieces
2 cups finely shredded green cabbage
2 cucumbers, halved, seeded, and cut
    in thin slices
2 carrots, cut into match-stick strips

Salad dressing:
    ½ cup onions, chopped fine
    4 tablespoons oil
    1 teaspoon ground chili powder
    1 tablespoon white vinegar
    Salt to taste
    ½ cup peanut butter
    1 cup water
    1 teaspoon sugar

DIRECTIONS.   *Bring a large pot of
water to a rapid boil. Maintain the water
at a boil and cook beansprouts,
beans, and cabbage as follows:
Place the beansprouts in a strainer,
immerse in boiling water 1 minute,
remove, rinse in cold water, and
drain. Cook the beans and cabbage
in same way for 6 and 4 minutes
respectively.
Place all the vegetables in a large
salad bowl, toss with dressing, and
serve at room temperature.*

DRESSING.   *Sauté onions in*
oil until limp, add chili powder,
white vinegar, salt, peanut butter,
water, and sugar. Stir to a smooth
paste over low flame. Simmer 1
minute.
THE SERVING.   *Cool salad dressing*
to room temperature and serve over
salad. Other suitable vegetables in this
salad are shredded lettuce and
spinach.

SATE PEANUT SAUCE
Makes 2 cups

INGREDIENTS.
¼ cup onion or shallots, chopped
   fine
2 cloves garlic, chopped fine
2 tablespoons oil
⅓ cup peanut butter
2 teaspoons ground chili powder
1 teaspoon turmeric powder
1 teaspoon brown sugar
1½ cup water
1 tablespoon lime juice
1 tablespoon dark soy
½ teaspoon grated fresh ginger

DIRECTIONS.   *Sauté onions or shal-*
lots and garlic in oil until
limp. Add the rest of the ingredients
and stir to a smooth paste over low
flame. Simmer 10 minutes.
Serve at room temperature as a
dipping sauce for sates.
This sauce can be prepared in
advance and kept in covered jar in
the refrigerator for 1 week or so. If
sauce has thickened, add water,
stir to a smooth paste, and serve.

CHAPTER TEN
VIETNAMESE
BARBECUED
MEAT

Vietnam stretches along the coast of the peninsula extending from China into the South China sea. It needs little introduction to the world, but its delicate cooking has until now been almost unknown except in France. The background of this elusive cuisine is historical.

Vietnam was part of the Chinese empire for over 1000 years before establishing itself as an independent nation. Chinese and Malays have formed part of its population for centuries. This has influenced the cuisine through the addition of noodles in soup, curries, and the use of coconut as flavoring. The French, with their flair for making sauces, soups, and cooking with fresh vegetables, further refined Vietnamese cooking during their rule. These influences combined with the produce of rich paddy fields and gardens, give rise to a distinctive Vietnamese cuisine. The cooking is light and refreshing using fresh ingredients such as bamboo shoots, leafy lettuce, Chinese parsley, mint leaves, shallots, scallions, lemon, and lime. Through all the flavors one finds the ever-present native seasoning, Nuoc Mam sauce.

Nuoc Mam, a clear light brown liquid, has the same seasoning function as salt or soy sauce in other parts of the world. It is very like light soy sauce in texture and saltiness, but as it is made by the fermentation of fresh fish and salt rather than soy beans, it has a slight flavor of the sea. This flavor is very elusive, and not fishy as one might think; it helps to bring out the flavor of food which salt alone does not. This fish sauce is available in Chinese grocery stores, sometimes as fish gravy sauce. In the recipes to follow, I have given light soy as a substitute whenever Nuoc Mam is not available.

The Vietnamese make some of the world's best soups and these form the base of many of their popular dishes. The rich broth is simmered from meat and bones, of which pork and chicken are favorites, and vegetables such as cabbage, turnips, or squash. When the soup is ready, the bones are discarded, and the meat, vegetables and soup are served alone, or over rice or noodles as a complete meal. A very popular version uses rice noodles with a pork soup. In this, crisp beansprouts, cucumber slices, lettuce, Chinese parsley, and mint leaves are put at the bottom of the individual rice bowls. Cooked rice noodles are placed on top of these, then the boiling broth with pieces of pork are ladled into it to make a delicious meal. Endless varieties of this vegetable–noodles or rice–broth combination are possible by using beef, fish, shrimps, or chicken. This is a very popular form of snack as it can be prepared quickly once you have the broth and garnishes at hand. In the market places, food stalls are fascinating places to linger watching the quick juggling act of the cook behind the counter dividing garnishes, adding noodles, and ladling the hot broth, then more garnishes, and so on.

Another popular form of Vietnamese food is the wrap-and-eat method. For this, cooked meat, rice or noodles, and garnishes of mint and Chinese parsley are layered on rice papers or lettuce leaves, wrapped into a loose bundle, dipped into Nuoc Mam, and eaten with the fingers. Although the meat can be thinly sliced beef or pork dunked briefly in a bubbling broth similar to the Chinese hot pot, the favorite wrapped meal is the lettuce leaf variety done with barbecued meat. The meat used here is barbecued ground pork, shrimps, or fish, seasoned and shaped into tiny sausagelike patties on skewers. After the patties are broiled, they are taken off the skewers and placed in a lettuce leaf together with rice, mint, and Chinese parsley, folded and dipped in a spicy version of Nuoc Mam sauce, and eaten. This is a complete meal in itself because rice, meat, and vegetables are all present in one bundle. An average person usually can eat three to four bundles, and no other dishes need be served.

If you are entertaining with the Vietnamese barbecue recipes that follow but do not want to use the wrap-and-eat method, just serve the skewered meat with rice seasoned with the Nuoc Mam sauce and a Vietnam-inspired salad. This is a combination of any of the following: lettuce, chives, cucumber, and beansprouts. Fresh mint and Chinese parsley are the herbs to use. Toss the salad in a Nuoc Mam sauce and add a squeeze of lime or lemon. The Vietnamese would end the meal with some Asian fruits such as bananas and pineapple, or peeled and cubed fresh sugar cane speared on bamboo skewers.

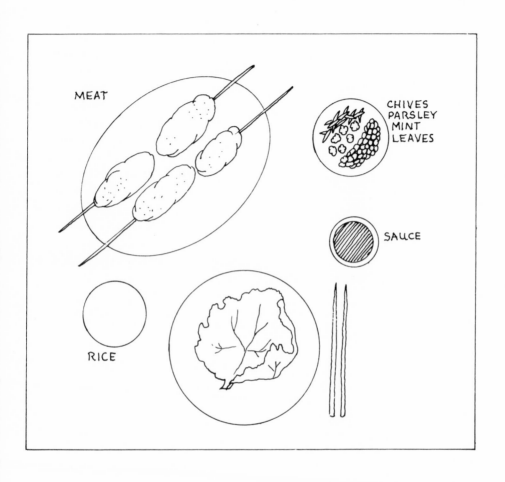

BARBECUED SKEWERED PORK PATTIES
Serves 4

INGREDIENTS.
2 pounds ground lean pork

Seasonings:
    2 cloves garlic, mashed
    1 teaspoon grated fresh ginger
    1 tablespoon sherry
    2 tablespoons light soy
    2 tablespoons oil
    1 teaspoon sugar
    Salt to taste

Wrap-and-eat garnishes:
    2 dozen whole fresh lettuce leaves,
      washed and drained
    2 cups raw white rice cooked accord-
      ing to page 45
    Spicy Nuoc Mam sauce page 77
    1 cup Chinese parsley leaves or
      chopped scallions
    1 cup fresh mint leaves or chopped
      celery leaves tops

Skewers
Charcoal grill, broiler, or hibachi

DIRECTIONS. *In a large bowl mix well ground pork, garlic, ginger, sherry, light soy, oil, sugar, and salt. Shape pork tightly into 2-inch balls. Squeeze each ball firmly into an elongated 3-inch sausage shape and thread skewer through its length. Set aside until you are ready to broil. Set the table by arranging bowls of lettuce leaves, rice cooled to room temperature, Nuoc Mam sauce, and parsley and mint within easy reach of each other.*

Prepare fire for broiling. Broil the pork patties 15 to 20 minutes either side till crisp and brown. Serve hot.
THE SERVING. *Each guest puts a lettuce leaf on his plate; place 1 tablespoon of rice on it, slide the pork patty off the skewer, and place the meat on top of the rice. Sprinkle with parsley and mint leaves, and fold the lettuce leaf together to wrap. Lift the bundle with fingers and dip into the Nuoc Mam sauce, then bite into a crisp tangy taste of pork and garnishes.*
Or sprinkle Nuoc Mam sauce on pork and rice before wrapping so you do not have to keep dipping into the sauce with each mouthful.

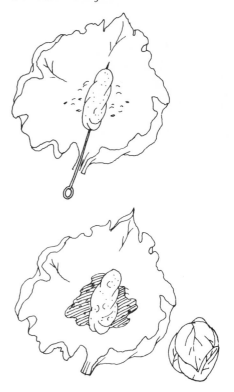

BARBECUED SKEWERED SHRIMP PATTIES
Serves 4

INGREDIENTS.
2 pounds fresh shrimps, shelled and
   chopped fine

Seasonings:
   1 egg
   2 scallions, chopped fine
   2 cloves garlic, mashed
   2 tablespoons fish sauce or light soy
   3 tablespoons oil
   1 teaspoon cornstarch
   ½ teaspoon sugar
   Salt and black papper to taste

Skewers
Charcoal grill, broiler, or hibachi
See preceding recipe for garnishes

DIRECTIONS.   *Chop shrimps finely
into a paste or put through a meat
grinder. Add egg, scallions, garlic, fish
sauce, oil, cornstarch, and sugar, salt,
and pepper. Mix well, and beat with a
wooden spoon to a smooth paste.
Shape shrimp paste tightly into 2-inch
balls, squeeze each ball firmly into an
elongated 3-inch sausage, and thread
skewer through its length. Prepare fire
for broiling and broil 10 minutes on
each side until crisp and brown.*
THE SERVING.   *Same procedure as
pork patties on page 75. Note: You may
substitute fish for shrimps for variety if
you wish. Made into smaller sausages,
with smaller skewers, these shrimp or fish
patties are excellent as cocktail tidbits.*

BARBECUED LEMON DUCK
Serves 4

INGREDIENTS.
one 4- to 5-pound duck, quartered
4 pieces scallions, chopped fine
1 teaspoon freshly grated ginger
2 teaspoons turmeric powder
2 tablespoons dark soy
1 teaspoon sugar
½ teaspoon grated lemon rind
Salt and black pepper
Lemon wedges

Charcoal grill, broiler, or hibachi

DIRECTIONS. *Marinate quartered
duck for 4 hours with scallions, ginger,
turmeric, dark soy, sugar, lemon rind,
salt, and pepper.
Prepare a fire for barbecuing.
Broil duck 3 to 4 inches from fire about
25 minutes on each side until done with
a crisp skin.
Serve hot.*
THE SERVING. *Serve with plain
rice seasoned with spicy Nuoc Mam
sauce, lemon wedges, and a green
salad made of lettuce, chives, cucumbers, and beansprouts.*

SPICY NUOC MAM SAUCE

INGREDIENTS.
1 cup fish sauce or light soy
6 slices fresh ginger ¼-inch thick,
  chopped fine
2 cloves garlic, mashed
1 teaspoon ground chili powder
3 tablespoons lemon juice
2 tablespoons sugar
¼ cup water

DIRECTIONS. *Mix all the ingredients well and divide into small bowls to
serve. This sauce can be kept in covered
jar for up to a week.*

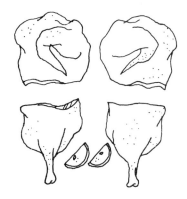

III
SHOPPING
GUIDE
FOR
INGREDIENTS

The recipes in this book span six Asian countries and use a variety of oriental ingredients. Most of these ingredients can be bought in the oriental section of the supermarket or gourmet shops. You will have no difficulty obtaining them in Chinese grocery shops. I have also given substitution, where possible, for relatively hard to find or perishable ingredients so that with the bare minimum of oriental ingredients (soy sauce and fresh ginger being the two that are indispensable in most recipes) you can prepare nearly all of the recipes given here. Glossary explanations in alphabetical order appear below:

BEANSPROUTS: *Sprouts of mung beans; available in oriental stores.. Many health food shops sell beans and directions for growing these yourself at home. Fresh ones are always preferred; however, if canned ones must be used, they should be rinsed in cold water and chilled for crispness before use. They do not keep.*

CHINESE CELERY CABBAGE: *Available in oriental food shops and many supermarkets; white broad stem with crinkled pale yellow leaves in one tight longish bundle. Chinese celery cabbage is different from ordinary cabbage. Wrapped, it can keep in the refrigerator for a week.*

81

CHINESE PARSLEY (CORI-ANDER) LEAVES: *Available in oriental grocery stores or Latin food stores (called cilantro); different from the curly parsley used in other types of cooking. Chinese parsley has flat indented leaves and a very distinct strong aroma. Use the fresh leaves only, in sauce or garnish. It can be substituted in small quantity by young celery leaves. Wrapped, it will keep in the refrigerator for 2 to 3 days.*

CHILIS: *Available in many grocery stores; the red and very hot variety sold in its dried form. Crush and grind chilis coarse to use, or use red pepper flakes or red chili powder. (Note: Pure red chili pepper powder is different from cayenne pepper or the mixed chili powder used in Chili con Carne or Mexican cooking.)*

HIBACHI: *Small Japanese charcoal grill for table barbecue.*

GINGER: *Fresh ginger root. Available in many grocery stores and some supermarkets. The fresh root has no substitute; dry ginger powder does not have the same taste. The roots can keep for months if peeled and immersed in sherry in a covered jar in the refrigerator. It can be replaced in Asian barbecues, if necessary, by garlic, shallots, or scallions.*

HOISIN SAUCE: *Available in any oriental food store and supermarket specialty sections; thick sweet reddish sauce made from soy beans and spices. Hoisin sauce comes in a bottle or can. It will keep in a covered jar in the refrigerator for 1 year.*

HORSERADISH (GREEN): *Available in Japanese food stores (called "wasabi"); hot, tart paste used in the Japanese recipes for eating with broiled meat. Green horseradish comes as a green powder and keeps forever. Make it into a thick paste with a little hot water just before use. English mustard powder may be used as a substitute.*

MARINADE: *Any sauce made from spices, herbs, and soy sauce for seasoning meat or food before cooking. Marinades vary from recipe to recipe.*

MINT LEAVES: *Available in many grocery stores; these fresh leaves are used in Vietnamese cooking for flavoring and garnish. There is no substitute for fresh mint although in the Vietnamese recipes it can be replaced by thinly shredded fresh lemon or lime leaves, or celery leaves.*

NUOC MAM (FISH SAUCE): *Vietnamese seasoning liquid similar to soy sauce made from fermented fish and salt. Read more about it on page 77. Light soy sauce may be substituted.*

OIL: *Either peanut or vegetable oil. Do not use olive oil or lard for the recipes given here.*

RICE: *Long grain raw white rice only in these recipes.*

RICE WINE OR SHERRY: *Rice wine is the Chinese kind made from fermented rice and is tea colored. Substitute with cooking sherry or drinking sake.*

SAKE WINE: *Available in most liquor stores. There are two kinds of sake: the pale not-as-sweet drinking sake, and the darker sweet mirin sake. The sweet Japanese sake (mirin) is used for cooking here. Substitute with cooking sherry, but use a bit less and add some sugar. Read more about sake on page 55.*

SEAWEEDS: *Available in Japanese food stores and used in Japanese cooking. Buy the roasted crisp brown sheets called Nori, sold by the packet. They will keep a long time in a covered jar.*

SESAME OIL: *Available in health food shops and sections of supermarkets; viscous oil made from sesame seeds and used for seasoning. Sesame oil has a very strong sesame flavor. It will keep for a long time.*

SESAME SEEDS: *Available in oriental and health food stores; roasted white sesame seeds used in Japanese and Korean cooking. The seeds can be toasted in a dry skillet over a flame or roasted in the oven until light brown.*

SHALLOTS: *Available in most food stores and supermarkets; small brown cloves of the onion family. Substitute with scallions, garlic, or onions.*

SHERRY: *Pale dry or cooking sherry for use in seasoning.*

SNOW PEA PODS: *Available in oriental and gourmet food shops fresh or frozen; these are fresh crisp green pea pods. Use fresh, if possible.*

SOY SAUCE: *Available in supermarket and oriental food shops; brown salty oriental seasoning liquid made from fermented soy beans. Soy sauce is the most common Asian cooking ingredient and each country makes its own. For the recipes in this book, three kinds are called for: the Chinese soy sauces which come in two types—the thicker, dark soy, and the thinner light soy; use these for all the recipes that specify either dark or light. The third kind is the Japanese soy sauce used in its cooking which can be replaced by the Chinese dark. In the event your market carries only one variety, it can be used as a substitute for the others. Keeps for a long time.*

83

STAR ANISE: *Available in oriental food shops; a dry brown star-shaped spice, licorice flavor. Star anise will keep forever in a covered jar. Substitute with anise extract in small amount.*

TEA: *For Asian dinners, only Chinese or Japanese tea. Pour boiling water over tea, steep for 10 minutes before pouring. Serve without milk or sugar.*

TURMERIC: *Available in all supermarkets in spice section; yellow powdery spice used in Indonesian cooking for both coloring and seasoning. Turmeric keeps forever.*

CHINESE TURNIPS (JAPANESE RADISH): *The oriental kind and very different from the common type found in the supermarkets. White, longish, and with green tops and a very distinct flavor. Keeps for one week when wrapped and kept in the refrigerator.*

WHITE VINEGAR: *The distilled white kind. Do not use wine or cider vinegar.*

INDEX

Angel Pot, 48
Appetizers, 14, 76
Asparagus, 59

Bamboo shoots, 53, 72
Banana, 73
Banana leaves
  for broiled fish, 68
  to cover skewer ends, 14
  for rice dishes, 63, 69
Bancha, 54
Barbecued Lemon Duck, 77
Barbecued Skewered Pork Patties, 26, 75
Barbecued Skewered Shrimp Patties, 76
Barbecued Spareribs, 43. *See also* Spareribs
Barley water, 48
Basting sauce, 38, 40, 45, 54, 55. *See also* Marinades
Beans, 63, 70
Beansprouts, 81
  in Gado-Gado Salad, 11, 63, 70
  in Mongolian fire grill, 29, 33
  in Vietnamese salad, 77
Beef
  for grilled slices, 26

in Japanese yakimonos, 11, 53, 54, 56
in Korean grilled meat, 11, 13
in Mongolian fire grill, 10, 30
for sate, 11, 63
selecting for barbecue method, 15
timetable, 25
Beef chuck, 31, 50
Beef flank steak, 15, 31, 50, 66
Beef Sate, 66
Beef short ribs, 12, 15, 48, 51
Beef sirloin, 15, 31, 50, 56
Beef tenderloin, 15, 31, 32, 47, 56
Beef Teriyaki, 11, 26, 56
Beer, 47, 53, 62
Beverages. *See* Barley water; Beer; Ginseng tea; Green tea; Rice water; Tea
Bread, 34, 35
Broccoli, 41
Broiled Beef Teriyaki, 26, 56
Broiled Chicken, 41
Broiled Chicken Yakitori, 57
Broiled Fish in Banana Leaves, 26, 69
Broiled Fish Yaki, 26, 58
Broiled Vegetables on Skewers, 59
Broiling, simple, 12, 15
Bul Kogi, 13, 48, 50

Cabbage, 11, 47, 48, 63, 70, 73
Carrots, 53, 70
Carving, roast suckling pig, 45. *See also* Slicing
Celery, 44
Charcoal, 12
Chicken
    broiled, 26
    in Chinese roast meat, 10, 37, 38
    in Korean grilled meat, 11, 47, 51
    in Mongolian dinner, 31
    for sate, 63
    selecting for barbecue method, 15
    spit broiling, 12
    timetable, 25
    for Vietnamese broth, 73
    in yakimonos, 11, 54
Chicken livers, 57
Chicken with scallions. *See* Chicken Yakitori
Chicken Yakitori, 11, 14, 54, 56
Chili powder, 11, 62
Chilis, 82
Chinese broiled chicken, 14
Chinese celery cabbage, 48, 52, 81
Chinese dinner menu, 26
Chinese parsley leaves, 11, 29, 62, 73, 75, 82
Chinese regional cuisine, 37
Chinese roast meat, 10, 37–46
Chinese salad, 26, 38, 41, 42, 43, 46
Chinese salad dressing, 44
Chinese Snow Pea Pods and Celery Salad, 44
Chives, 71
Cilantro. *See* Chinese parsley
Coconut, 72
Coconut milk, 62, 63
Cold barbecue supper, 38
Cold Rice Longtongs, 11, 26, 63–64, 65, 66, 67, 69

"Cooked meats" shops, 37, 38
Cooking procedures, 35, 63. *See also* Broiling; Slicing
Coriander. *See* Chinese parsley
Cucumbers, 11, 44, 47, 52, 53, 63, 70, 77
Curries, 62, 63, 72

Desserts. *See* Menus
Dipping sauce, 63
Duck
    in Chinese roast meat, 10, 37, 38
    recipes, 40, 77
    selecting for barbecue method, 15
    spit broiling, 12–13
    timetable, 25

Egg, 48
Eggplant, 34, 59
Equipment, 10, 21–24, 29, 34. *See also* Hibachi; Skewers

Fire, 21–25
Fish
    broiled, 68
    dry, 48, 53
    ground, 11, 73
    method for, 15
    timetable, 25
    yaki, 11, 26, 54, 58
    See also Mackerel; Pompano; Sea bass; Snapper; Tuna
Fish sauce. *See* Nuoc Mam
Fish Yaki, 54
Five-spice powder, 45
Fruit, 26, 35, 51, 53
Fuel, 22

Gado-Gado Salad, 11, 26, 63, 65, 66, 67, 70

Genghis Khan dinner. *See* Mongolian fire grill
Ginger, 7, 10, 11, 38, 41, 42, 51, 52, 57, 58, 62, 65, 66, 71, 77, 81, 82
Ginseng, 48
Ginseng tea, 48
Glaze, for teriyaki, 55, 56
Goat, in Mongolian fire grill, 29
Green horseradish, 11. *See also* Horseradish paste; Horseradish powder
Green pepper, 34, 59
Green tea, 53, 54, 55
Grilled Beef Slices, 26
Grilled Korean Short Ribs, 51
Ground beef, 15
Ground meat, for Vietnamese barbecue, 11

Hibachi, 11, 13, 21, 34, 54, 82
History of Asian barbecue, 9–10
Hoisin sauce, 10, 38, 40, 42, 43, 45, 46, 82
Horseradish paste, 53, 55, 58, 82
Horseradish powder, 56
Hwa Ru, 48

Indonesian Broiled Fish, 14
Indonesian dinner, 26
Indonesian salads, 63. *See also* Gado-Gado Salad
Indonesian sates, definition, 11, 14, 62–65

Japanese dinner, 26
Japanese radish. *See* Turnips, Chinese

Kabob cooking, 62

Kim Chee Salad, 11, 26, 47, 48, 51, 52
Kobe beef, 53
Korean dinner, 26
Korean grilled meat, definition, 10, 47, 48
Korean salad. *See* Kim Chee Salad

Lamb
    ground, 15
    leg of, 15, 65
    for Mongolian fire grill, 10, 11, 29, 30, 32, 33
    for sate, 11, 26, 65
    selecting for barbecue, 15
    slicing, 31
Lamb chops, 15
Lamb Sate, 26, 65
Leeks, 10, 29, 33
Lemon, 62, 72, 73, 77
Lettuce, 26, 71, 72, 73, 75, 77
Lime, 62, 71, 72, 73
Liver, 38
Longtongs. *See* Cold Rice Longtongs

Mackerel, 58
Mandoo, 48
Marinades, 10, 11, 29, 33, 38, 41, 42, 47, 50, 51, 56, 57, 58, 59, 63, 65, 66, 67, 82
Meat, choosing for barbecue, 15
Meat patties, Vietnamese, 14, 26
Menus, 26, 54
Methods for barbecuing, 12–14, 15. *See also* Broiling, simple; Cooking procedures; Slicing
Mint, 11, 73, 75, 82
Mirin sake, 55, 83
Mongolian dinner, 26
Mongolian fire grill, definition, 10, 13, 29–31

Mongolian fire grill *(continued)*
  in menu, 26
  method, 31–32, 35
  recipes, 33–35
  table setting, 36–37
Mongolian Fire Pot, 30
Monosodium glutamate, 53
Mung beans. *See* Beansprouts
Mushrooms, 48, 53, 59
Mustard, 53, 55
Mutton
  in Mongolian cuisine, 10, 29, 30, 31
  selecting for barbecue, 15
  slicing, 31, 32, 33

Noodles, 72, 73
  rice noodles, 73
Nori. *See* Seaweeds
Nuoc Mam sauce, 11, 72, 73, 75, 76,
  77, 82

Onion, 34

Parsley, 33, 35. *See also* Chinese par-
  sley
Peanut sauce, 63, 65, 66, 67, 71
Peanuts, ground, 11, 62, 63, 66, 70
Persimmons, 53
Pickled vegetables. *See* Kim Chee
  Salad
Pickles, 53
Pig, whole, spit broiling for, 12. *See
  also* Suckling pig
Pineapple, 73
Plain White Rice, 45. *See also* Rice
Pompano, 58, 68
Pork
  in Chinese roast meat, 10, 37, 38
  ground, 11, 26, 73, 75

in Japanese yakimonos, 53
for Korean grilled meat, 47, 51
roast, 12, 13, 42
for sate, 11, 63
selecting for barbecue, 15
slicing, 32
tenderloin, 15, 25
timetable, 25
for Vietnamese broth, 73
Pork chops, 15
Preparing meat for barbecue. *See*
  Slicing meat

Radish, 53
Rice, 26, 30, 34, 35, 38, 41, 42, 43, 45,
  46, 47, 48, 51, 53, 62, 63, 68, 69,
  73, 75, 77. *See also* Cold Rice
  Longtongs; Vinegared Rice
Rice vinegar, 53
Rice water, 48
Rice wine, 29, 33, 83
Rijst-tafel, 62
Roast Duck, 40. *See also* Duck
Roast meat shops. *See* "Cooked
  meats" shops   .
Roast Pork Strips, 42. *See also* Pork;
  Pork tenderloin
Roast Suckling Pig, 45. *See also* Suck-
  ling pig
Round table broiling, 13, 15

Sake, 11, 53, 54, 55, 56, 57, 58, 60, 83
Salad. *See* Chinese salad; Gado-Gado
  Salad; Indonesian salads; Kim
  Chee Salad; Spinach and Sesame
  Seed Salad; Vietnamese salad
Salad dressings. *See* Chinese Snow
  Pea Pods and Celery Salad;
  Gado-Gado Salad with Peanut
  Dressing; Kim Chee Salad; Spin-
  ach and Sesame Seed Salad

Sambal sauce, 63
Sates. *See* Indonesian sates
Sauces. *See* Basting sauce; Dipping sauce; Marinades; Sambal sauce; Seasoning sauce
Scallions, 33, 35, 48, 59, 72, 75
Scallops, 58
Sea bass, 68
Seafood, 53. *See also* Scallops; Shrimp
Seasoning sauce, 38, 40, 45
Sea trout, 15, 68
Seaweeds, 48, 53, 83
Serving, 30, 35, 47, 49, 53, 55, 64, 67
Sesame oil, 38, 44, 52, 56, 83
Sesame seeds, 11, 47, 48, 50, 51, 83
Shallots, 83
Sherry, 83
Shrimp
  ground, 11, 73, 76
  in Korean grilled meat, 11, 47, 48, 51
  in Mongolian dinner, 31
  for sate, 11, 63, 67
  selecting for barbecue method, 15
  timetable, 25
  in yakimonos, 54, 58
Shrimp paste, 62, 76
Shrimp Sate, 67
Sincha, 54
Skewer broiling, 13–14, 15, 18, 19, 57, 58, 63, 65, 66, 67, 75
Slicing
  choosing method, 16
  techniques, 16–19, 31, 32, 51
  for yakimonos, 54
Snapper, 15, 68
Snow pea pods, 83. *See also* Chinese Snow Pea Pods and Celery Salad
Soup, 48, 51, 73
Soy bean paste, 53
Soy sauce, 10, 11, 29, 33, 38, 48, 62,

  63, 83
  dark, 38, 40, 41, 43, 45, 47, 50, 51, 54, 65, 68, 71, 81, 83
  Japanese, 11, 53, 54, 57, 58, 59, 61, 83
  light, 44, 73, 76, 77, 83
Spareribs
  barbecued, 26, 43
  in Chinese roast meat, 10, 12, 37, 38
  spit broiling for, 13, 15
  timetable, 25
Spinach, 29, 33, 61, 71. *See also* Spinach and Sesame Seed Salad
Spinach and Sesame Seed Salad, 11, 26, 54, 55, 56, 57, 58, 61
Spit broiling, 12–13, 15, 38, 40, 46
Squabs, 37
Squash, 48, 59
Squids, 37, 54
Star anise, 33, 40, 84
Stir-fry dishes, 35, 62
Strawberries, 53
String beans, 59
Suckling pig, 10, 12, 37, 38, 45
Sugar cane, 73

Table settings, 36, 39. *See also* Serving
Tamarind, 62
Tea, 26, 35, 47, 84. *See also* Green tea
Teriyaki, 11, 54, 55
Teriyaki sauce, 55
Timetable, 24, 25
Tongue, 37
Tuna, 58
Turmeric, 11, 62, 71, 73, 84
Turnips, Chinese, 47, 52, 84

Vegetables, 29, 30, 34, 38, 53, 59, 72, 73

Venison, 10, 15, 29, 30, 31, 32, 33
Vietnamese barbecued lemon duck, 44, 77
Vietnamese barbecued meat, definition, 11, 72–74
Vietnamese dinner, 26
Vietnamese salad, 73
Vinegar, white, 84
Vinegar dressing, 60
Vinegared rice, 26, 54, 55, 56, 57, 58, 60

Wasabi. *See* Horseradish
Watchman's dinner, 48
Watercress, 10, 29, 33

Wok, 34
Wrap and broil method, 14
"Wrap and eat." *See* Vietnamese barbecued meat
"Wrap and eat" garnishes, 75

Yaki cooking. *See* Yakimonos
Yakimonos, definition, 11, 53–55. *See also* Beef; Chicken; Fish; Vegetables
Yakitori, 19, 54

Zucchini, 59